SIGMUND FREUD

The work of Sigmund Freud has penetrated almost every area of literary theory and cultural studies, as well as contemporary culture. Pamela Thurschwell explains and contextualises psychoanalytic theory and its meaning for modern thinking. This updated second edition explores developments and responses to Freud's work, including:

- Tracing contexts and developments of Freud's work over the course of his career;
- Exploring paradoxes and contradictions in his writing;
- Focusing on psychoanalysis as an interpretative strategy, paying special attention to its impact on literary and cultural theory;
- Examining the recent backlash against Freud and arguing for the continued relevance of psychoanalysis.

Encouraging and preparing readers to approach Freud's original texts, this guide ensures that readers of all levels will find Freud accessible, challenging and of continued relevance.

Pamela Thurschwell is a Senior Lecturer in English at the University of Sussex. She is the author of *Literature, Technology and Magical Thinking, 1880–1920*.

ROUTLEDGE CRITICAL THINKERS

Series Editor: Robert Eaglestone, Royal Holloway, University of London

Routledge Critical Thinkers is a series of accessible introductions to key figures in contemporary critical thought.

With a unique focus on historical and intellectual contexts, the volumes in this series examine important theorists':

- significance
- motivation
- key ideas and their sources
- impact on other thinkers.

Concluding with extensively annotated guides to further reading, *Routledge Critical Thinkers* are the student's passport to today's most exciting critical thought.

Also available in the series:

For further information on this series visit:
www.routledgeliterature.com/books/series.

SIGMUND FREUD

Second edition

Pamela Thurschwell

Routledge
Taylor & Francis Group

LONDON AND NEW YORK

First edition published 2000 by Routledge
Second edition published 2009 by Routledge
2 Park Square, Milton Park, Abingdon, Oxon OX14 4RN

Simultaneously published in the USA and Canada
by Routledge
270 Madison Ave, New York, NY 10016

Routledge is an imprint of the Taylor & Francis Group, an informa business

Typeset in Perpetua by Taylor & Francis Books
Printed and bound in Great Britain by TJ International Ltd, Padstow, Cornwall

British Library Cataloguing in Publication Data
A catalogue record for this book is available from the British Library

Library of Congress Cataloging-in-Publication Data
Thurschwell, Pamela, 1966-
Sigmund Freud / by Pamela Thurschwell. – 2nd ed.
    p. cm. – (Routledge critical thinkers)
Includes bibliographical references and index.
    1. Psychoanalysis. 2. Freud, Sigmund, 1856-1939. 3. Psychoanalysis and
culture. I. Title.
      BF173.T555 2009
      150.19'52092–dc22
                              2008052641

ISBN10: 0-415-47368-3 (hbk)
ISBN10: 0-415-47369-1 (pbk)
ISBN10: 0-203-88806-5 (ebk)

ISBN13: 978-0-415-47368-2 (hbk)
ISBN13: 978-0-415-47369-9 (pbk)
ISBN13: 978-0-203-88806-3 (ebk)

CONTENTS

SERIES EDITOR'S PREFACE

The books in this series offer introductions to major critical thinkers who have influenced literary studies and the humanities. The *Routledge Critical Thinkers* series provides the books you can turn to first when a new name or concept appears in your studies.

Each book will equip you to approach a key thinker's original texts by explaining their key ideas, putting then into context and, perhaps most important, showing you why the thinker is considered to be significant. The emphasis is on concise, clearly written guides which do not presuppose specialist knowledge. Although the focus is on particular figures, the series stresses that no critical thinker ever existed in a vacuum but, instead, emerged from a broader intellectual, cultural and social history. Finally, these books act as a bridge between you and the thinkers' original texts: not replacing them but rather complementing what they wrote. In some cases, volumes consider small clusters of thinkers working in the same area, developing similar ideas or influencing each other.

These books are necessary for a number of reasons. In his 1997 autobiography, *Not Entitled*, the literary critic Frank Kermode wrote of a time in the 1960s:

> On beautiful summer lawns, young people lay together all night, recovering from their daytime exertions and listening to a troupe of Balinese musicians.

> Under their blankets or their sleeping bags, they would chat drowsily about the gurus of the time ... What they repeated was largely hearsay; hence my lunchtime suggestion, quite impromptu, for a series of short, very cheap books offering authoritative but intelligible introductions to such figures.

There is still a need for 'authoritative and intelligible introductions'. But this series reflects a different world from the 1960s. New thinkers have emerged and the reputations of others have risen and fallen as new research has developed. New methodologies and challenging ideas have spread through the arts and humanities. The study of literature is no longer – if it ever was – simply the study and evaluation of poems, novels and plays. It is also the study of ideas, issues and difficulties which arise in any literary text and in its interpretation. Other arts and humanities subjects have changed in analogous ways.

With these changes, new problems have emerged. The ideas and issues behind these radical changes in the humanities are often presented without reference to wider contexts or as theories which you can simply 'add on' to the texts you read. Certainly, there's nothing wrong with picking out selected ideas or using what comes to hand – indeed, some thinkers have argued that this is, in fact, all we can do. However, it is sometimes forgotten that each new idea comes from the pattern and development of somebody's thought and it is important to study the range and context of their ideas. Against theories 'floating in space' the *Routledge Critical Thinkers* series places key thinkers and their ideas firmly back in their context.

More than that, these books reflect the need to go back to the thinkers' own texts and ideas. Every interpretation of an idea, even the most seemingly innocent one, offers you its own 'spin', implicitly or explicitly. To read only books *on* a thinker, rather than texts *by* that thinker, is to deny yourself the chance of making up your own mind. Sometimes what makes a significant figure's work hard to approach is not so much its style or content as the feeling of not knowing where to start. The purpose of these books is to give you a 'way in' by offering an accessible overview of these thinkers' ideas and works and by guiding your further reading, starting with each thinker's own texts. To use a metaphor from the philosopher Ludwig Wittgenstein (1889–1951), these books are ladders, to be thrown away after you have climbed to the next level. Not only, then, do they equip you to approach new ideas, but also they empower you, by leading you back to the theorist's own texts and encouraging you to develop your own informed opinions.

Finally, these books are necessary because, just as intellectual needs have changed, education systems round the world – the contexts in which introductory books are usually read – have changed radically, too. What was suitable for the minority higher education systems of the 1960s is not suitable for the larger, wider, more diverse, high-technology education systems of the twenty-first century. These changes call not just for new, up-to-date introductions but new methods of presentation. The presentational aspects of *Routledge Critical Thinkers* have been developed with today's students in mind.

Each book in the series has a similar structure. It begins with a section offering an overview of the life and ideas of the featured thinkers and explain why they are important. The central section of each book discusses the thinkers' key ideas, their context, evolution, and reception; in the books that deal with more than one thinker, they also explain and explore the influence of each on each. The volumes conclude with a survey of the impact of the thinker or thinkers, out-lining how their ideas have been taken up and developed by others. In addition, there is a detailed final section suggesting and describing books for further reading. This is not a 'tacked on' section but an integral part of each volume. In the first part of this section you will find brief descriptions of the thinkers' key works, then, following it, information on the most useful critical works and, in some cases, on relevant websites. This section will guide you in your reading, enabling you to follow your interests and develop your own projects. Throughout each book, references are given in what is known as the Harvard system (the author and the date of a work are cited in the text and you can look up the full details in the bibliography at the back). This offers a lot of information in very little space. The books also explain technical terms and use boxes to describe events or ideas in more detail, away from the main emphasis of the discussion. 'Boxes' are also used at times to highlight definitions of terms frequently used or coined by a thinker. In this way the boxes serve as a kind of glossary, easily identified when flicking through the book.

The thinkers in the series are 'critical' for three reasons. First, they are examined in the light of subjects which involve criticism: princi-pally literary studies or English and cultural studies, but also other disciplines which rely on the criticism of books, ideas, theories and unquestioned assumptions. Second, they are critical because studying their work will provide you with a 'toolkit' for your own informed critical reading and thought, which will make you critical. Third, these thinkers are critical because they are crucially important: they deal with ideas and questions which can overturn conventional under-standings of the world, of texts, of everything we take for granted, leaving us with a deeper understanding of what we already knew and with new ideas.

No introduction can tell you everything. However, by offering a way into critical thinking, this series hopes to begin to engage you in an activity which is productive, constructive and potentially life-changing.

ACKNOWLEDGEMENTS

The lines from W.H. Auden, 'In Memory of Sigmund Freud', are reproduced by permission of Faber & Faber Ltd. I would also like to thank everyone who has supported me through the writing of this book, and everyone who told me that they had a really weird dream last night, particularly Jim Endersby.

WHY FREUD?

Sigmund Freud's impact on how we think, and how we think about how we think, has been enormous. The twentieth century has been called the Freudian century, and whatever the twenty-first century chooses to believe about the workings of the human mind, it will be, on some level, indebted to Freud. (Of course, this may be a debt that involves reacting against his ideas as much as it involves subscribing to them.) Freud's theory, psychoanalysis, suggested new ways of understanding, amongst other things, love, hate, childhood, family relations, civilisation, religion, sexuality, fantasy and the conflicting emotions that make up our daily lives. Today we all live in the shadow of Freud's innovative and controversial concepts. In their scope and subsequent impact Freud's writings embody a core of ideas that amount to more than the beliefs of a single thinker. Rather, they function like myths for our culture; taken together, they present a way of looking at the world that has been powerfully transformative. The poet W.H. Auden probably put it best when he wrote of Freud: 'if often he was wrong and, at times, absurd,/to us he is no more a person/now but a whole climate of opinion/under which we conduct our different lives' ('In Memory of Sigmund Freud', Auden 1976: 275).

But what is this strange 'climate of opinion', psychoanalysis? How did a turn-of-the-century Viennese doctor, who may now seem to us often wrong and sometimes absurd, become so central to our vision of ourselves as thinking, feeling beings in the twenty-first century? And if psychoanalysis really is 'often wrong and sometimes absurd', why read it at all? While providing a compact introduction to Freud's life, important concepts and key texts, this study also aims to offer some answers to these wider questions. Putting psychoanalysis in context theoretically and historically will allow us to understand better why, when we look around us, psychoanalytic ideas are pervasive, not only in university bookshops and psychiatric offices, but also in newspapers, movies, modern art exhibits, romantic fiction, self-help books and television talk shows – in short, everywhere where we find our culture reflecting back images of ourselves. Modern literary criticism has been particularly influenced by psychoanalysis, and this book will foreground that fact in two ways: by examining Freud's readings of literature and subsequent critics' uses of Freud; and by introducing Freud's own writings, using the techniques of literary criticism.

Three key concepts are helpful to keep in mind when beginning to read Freud: sexuality, memory and interpretation. By thinking about the sometimes conflicting and complicated meanings of these three common words we can cover a lot of psychoanalytic ground. Psychoanalysis provides both a theory of the history of the individual mind – its early development, its frustrations and desires (which include sexual, or what Freud calls libidinal, desires) – and a set of specific therapeutic techniques for recalling, interpreting and coming to terms with that individual history. Sex, memory, interpretation – psychoanalysis shows how these three apparently disparate terms are connected to each other.

Freud's name is indissolubly linked with sex. His theories of the mind emphasise the early development of sexuality in the infant child, and the adult psychological illnesses that emerge in the conflict between individual sexual desires and society's demands not to indulge in these unruly urges. It is for his ideas about the importance of sexuality that Freud is perhaps most famous (some would say notorious). Memory, like sex, is also a straightforward concern of Freud's; psychoanalysis calls on individuals to recall the childhood events and fantasies that shaped their personalities. But why stress this other term, interpretation?

To answer this question, I'd like to explore one widespread image of Freud as sex-obsessed. One popular (and mistaken) assumption about psychoanalysis is that it claims that everything refers finally to sexual desire; even if you're sure you're thinking about something else, a Freudian will insist that you're really thinking about sex. A patient lying on a couch tells an analyst that he dreamt last night about a train going through a tunnel. Aha! the analyst exclaims, stroking his long white beard. The train is a phallic symbol and the tunnel a vaginal one: you were fantasising about having sex with your mother.

We might imagine this scene taking place in a movie making fun of psychoanalysis. But even in this parodic example of what Freud would call 'wild analysis', we can recognise the central importance of interpretation to the analytic scene. The analyst sees the elements of the patient's dream in terms of what they symbolise; he *reads* and *interprets* them (or in this case, one might say, forces an interpretation upon them). Psychoanalysis is a theory of reading first and foremost; it suggests that there are always more meanings to any statement than there appear to be at first glance. For the analyst a train is never just a train. To employ some of the metaphors that are so central to Freud's terminology, one critical goal of psychoanalysis is towards searching *behind* and *below* the surface content of the language of our everyday life. Many of Freud's important early books, *The Interpretation of Dreams* (1900), *The Psychopathology of Everyday Life* (1901), and *Jokes and their Relation to the Unconscious* (1905) read like primers on how to interpret the deeper meanings of various communications and miscommunications that pass through the individual mind and between people: random thoughts, dreams, jokes, slips of the tongue, moments of forgetting, etc.

Knowing how to read a dream, daydream or slip of the tongue – to unlock its symbolism and understand its multiple meanings – is a process not unlike reading a novel or a poem. When we read literature critically, we discover many different layers and meanings – some of which may contradict each other. Reading Freud's works, one must always be willing to immerse oneself in contradiction. He revises and rewrites his early theories in his later work. His body of psychoanalytic writings spans the period from the 1880s to his death in the late 1930s; often he contradicts one of his own earlier ideas or finds evidence to suggest he was wrong the first time round. Because of the length of time over which he wrote, and the breadth of his speculative and clinical thought, there are always different, often conflicting, positions to emphasise when reading Freud. This introduction to Freud sees these conflicts as a strength rather than a weakness of psychoanalytic thinking, and works through Freud's writings with an eye towards the productiveness of contradiction. Reading Freud properly means reading him carefully. Even when you think you know what he's going to say, he may surprise you.

The terrain that psychoanalysis explores is that of the individual **psyche**.

PSYCHE

Originating from Greek myth, the word 'psyche' originally referred to the soul. Freud's German *die Seele* translates to soul, but the standard English translation of Freud's work (the series of volumes known as the Standard Edition) downplays the religious context of soul so that psyche becomes the mental apparatus as it is defined in contrast to the body or the soma. (A somatic illness is one that is caused by bodily rather than mental factors.)

The key to the psyche that Freud asks us to read, the storehouse of conflicting energies and disguised desires, is the individual's **unconscious**. For Freud every thought is unconscious before it is conscious: 'Psychoanalysis regarded everything mental as being in the first instance unconscious; the further quality of "consciousness" might also be present, or again it might be absent' (Freud 1925a: 214).

UNCONSCIOUS

The unconscious, for Freud, can be defined in several different ways. It is, in one definition, the storehouse of instinctual desires and needs. Childhood wishes and memories live on in unconscious life, even if they have been erased from consciousness. The unconscious is, in a sense, the great waste-paper basket of the mind – the trash that never gets taken out: 'in mental life nothing which has once been formed can perish ... everything is somehow preserved and ... in suitable circumstances ... it can once more be brought to light' (Freud 1930: 256). In another of Freud's definitions, the unconscious is understood dynamically, as a system engaged in an ongoing conflict with consciousness; the unconscious material of the mind is kept out of consciousness via repression (see **repression** on p. 21).

We will return to and refine our definition of this central psycho-analytic concept later, in our discussion of Freud's topography (mapping) of the mind in Chapter 5, but this definition of the unconscious will suffice as an initial explanation.

Besides defining certain key psychoanalytic concepts, before we can grasp Freud's ideas it is necessary to understand something about how his theories formed and changed in response to the surrounding intellectual and political climate. The rest of this introductory chapter will provide a short history of Freud's life and cultural circumstances. The next short chapter will provide a roughly chronological account of the early ideas that led to his initial development of psychoanalytic theory and practice.

LIFE AND CONTEXT

What then were the historical and personal circumstances that helped fashion the man Sigmund Freud and the theory and clinical practice, psychoanalysis, that is inseparable from his name? Freud was born on 6 May 1856 in the Moravian town of Freiburg. He was the son of a Jewish wool merchant, Jacob Freud, and his third wife, Amalie. When Freud was four his family moved to Vienna, where he would continue to live and work for the next seventy-nine years before being forced to leave because of the threat of Nazi persecution in 1938. In that year he and his family emigrated to England, where he died on 23 September 1939.

Outwardly Freud's life was not terribly eventful until his family's somewhat dramatic escape from Vienna. If Freud created a revolution with his new ideas about sexuality and unconscious desires, the battles he fought were conceptual ones rather than active ones. It is fair to say that he took the intellectual and cultural atmosphere he grew up in and made something new with it, yet he also worked within its limits.

The Vienna of the late nineteenth century was a contradictory city. Although it was home to sophisticated, liberal ideas in its intellectual café society, and its art, music and literature, by the turn of the century Vienna was also a city with deep economic problems. Recent historians have pointed out that the Vienna bourgeoisie was over-whelmingly Jewish. Although Jews made up only 10 per cent of the population of Vienna, more than half the doctors and lawyers in the city in 1890 were Jewish (Forrester 1997: 189). With cultural advantages came backlash. Antisemitism was also a part of life in Vienna. In his 'Autobiographical Study' Freud wrote of the consequence of encountering antisemitism in his career as a student: 'These first impressions at the University, however, had one consequence which was afterwards to prove important; for at an early age I was made familiar with the fate of being in the Opposition … The foundations were thus laid for a certain degree of independence of judgement' (Freud 1925a: 191). This sense of being in the opposition would stay with Freud for the rest of his life. In truth, there were, from the beginning, violent opponents of psychoanalytic ideas, but being in the opposition was also a stance that Freud relished: he enjoyed being the lone thinker, forging away at his revolutionary ideas without outside support. In fact Freud did not work entirely in isolation, and understanding the influences on him can help enhance our understanding of the scientific, historical and cultural ground from which psychoanalysis sprang.

As a boy Freud was intellectually precocious, learning many languages, including Greek, Latin, English, French and Hebrew. He began to read Shakespeare at the age of eight. He studied medicine at the University of Vienna from 1873 to 1881, although his initial interest was in zoological rather than human science. He claims in his 'Autobiographical Study': 'Neither at that time, nor indeed later in my career did I feel any particular predilection for the career of a doctor. I was moved, rather, by a sort of curiosity, which was, however, directed more towards human concerns than towards natural objects' (Freud 1925a: 190). From 1876 to 1882 he worked with the professor of physiology, Ernst Brücke (1819–92) in Brücke's Physiological Institute. Brücke was a believer in mechanism, the principle that physical and chemical causes could explain all life processes without reference to religious or other vitalistic causes. Consciousness itself could be explained through biological processes. Following on the mid-century discoveries of evolutionary theory – that humans, like other species of animals, had evolved and changed – nineteenth-century scientific and philosophical thought had embraced the concept that all life could be explained through the experimental methods of science. Freud began, like Brücke, as a mechanist and a believer in physical causes for mental diseases, but he soon came to believe in a distinct role for psychology in mental life, a role apart from strictly biological causes. Yet Freud never gave up his determinist belief in the principles of cause and effect. His theories indicated that every hysterical symptom he examined, every dream, every slip of the tongue, everything we say or think on a daily basis, has a cause. It may not always be possible to uncover the cause, but it is there.

Research was Freud's primary interest early in his medical career. He had no particular desire to practise medicine, but in 1882 he became engaged to Martha Bernays (1861–1951) and felt the economic pressures and responsibilities of a soon-to-be-married man planning on setting up a home and family. Practising medicine paid more than research, and Freud eventually moved from studying the spinal cords of fishes to studying the human central nervous system. He set up his own medical practice, specialising in the nervous diseases, as well as becoming a lecturer in neuropathology at the University of Vienna in 1885. Soon he began to treat the middle- and upper middle-class women patients whose hysterical illnesses led him to develop the theory of psychoanalysis. (See Chapter 1, 'Early theories', for more on hysteria and these early patients.)

Freud developed his radical ideas about nervous illness initially in *Studies on Hysteria*, a series of case histories he co-wrote with his colleague Joseph Breuer (1842–1925). He refined and changed the theory of psychoanalysis through the 1890s and published his first major psychoanalytic work, *The Interpretation of Dreams*, in 1900. The book sold slowly at first. Eventually, however, Freud's ideas began to pick up followers even as they simultaneously encountered resistance and sometimes outrage. Freud devoted his life to expanding and refining his theories and to establishing psychoanalysis as an institution. His first books are primarily concerned with questions of interpretation – *The Interpretation of Dreams* with dream symbolism, *Jokes and their Relation to the Unconscious* with the meanings of jokes and *The Psychopathology of Everyday Life* with the meanings of slips of the tongue, mistakes, forgotten words, etc. Freud's innovative ideas and methods of interpretation will be discussed in Chapter 2. But Freud was also convinced of the importance of sexual life and early childhood development, both to nervous illness and to everyone's growth into troubled or untroubled adulthood. His *Three Essays on the Theory of Sexuality* were published in 1905 and set the agenda for psychoanalysis's emphasis on sexual development, which is explored in detail in Chapter 3.

It would be mistaken to think that Freud was alone in his interest in sex as a central aspect of human behaviour at the time. At the end of the nineteenth century sexual behaviour, identities and relations emerged as an object of study, eventually becoming the discipline we now call sexology. Researchers such as Richard von Krafft-Ebing, Havelock Ellis and Magnus Hirschfeld began scrutinising and classifying the field of sexuality at approximately the same time as Freud. Like Freud, sexologists presumed that understanding sexual motivations and desires was important to understanding an individual's life and also to understanding society as a whole. Sexologists drew their ideas from many different disciplines, including anthropology, history and biology. They also helped develop a new way of thinking about medical cases by encouraging people to narrate their own sexual histories – the 'case study'.

Freud similarly drew the material for his theoretical works from his work with patients. His case histories – with their appealing nicknames, such as 'The Wolf Man', 'The Rat Man' and 'Little Hans' – often seem more like psychological thrillers than dry medical reports. They helped create a new genre of medical narrative, concerned not only with the story that the patient told about his or her own symptoms but with the way the patient told that story. The major case histories are described in Chapter 4.

From the mid-1910s onwards Freud attempted to formulate his theory of the mind into a coherent plot or project – he postulated the categories of the ego, id and super-ego to help explain the divisions he saw between different functions of the mind. (See pp. 45 and 80 for definitions of ego, id and super-ego.) Chapter 5 explores Freud's various mappings of the mind over his career.

Until his death in 1939 Freud continued writing on art, literature, war, death, fear, the methodology of psychoanalysis and the origins of culture, society and religion. Chapter 6 outlines Freud's major ideas about the structure of civilisation and society. He also wrote articles on specific works of art and artists (see 'The *Moses* of Michelangelo' and 'Leonardo da Vinci and a Memory of his Childhood') and on specific sexual pathologies (see 'Fetishism'). The influences that contributed to Freud's ideas were manifold. His theories were meant to explain all human psychology, but he formulated them in response to the historical times he lived in. For instance, after the devastating effects of World War I and the death of his favourite daughter, Sophie, he wrote *Beyond the Pleasure Principle* (1920), in which he explored the possibility of a universal drive towards death. Freud collected antiquities and was fascinated by archaeology, which fed into articles such as 'Delusions and Dreams in Jensen's *Gradiva*', a psychoanalytic reading of a short story about an archaeologist exploring the ruins of Pompeii. In the course of his writing career Freud takes the basic principles of psychoanalysis and applies them to culture, literature, art and society. But what exactly are these basic principles? They can be traced by examining the ways in which Freud's early theories developed. In the next chapter I will return to Freud's initial encounter with hysteria in the 1890s, to trace the ways in which psychoanalysis evolved in response to the stories told by patients about their illnesses.

PSYCHOANALYSIS: AN AUTOBIOGRAPHICAL THEORY?

Before ending this introductory chapter I want to say something more about Freud's own autobiographical relationship to his theories, as well as his personal relationships with the men and women who became the first psychoanalysts. As Freud refined his ideas about the causes of and cures for mental illness in the last decade of the nineteenth century and the first decade of the twentieth, interest in his theories began to grow, and followers began to accrue to this new clinical and theoretical practice, psychoanalysis. Freud was always concerned about the status of psychoanalysis as a discipline; he wanted it to have the authority of a science, and he saw his concepts as reflecting essential truths about how the mind worked in dynamic relations with memory and sexual desire.

Freud's personal relations were intimately bound up with the development of the status of psychoanalysis. Amongst his colleagues there was a strict, if unwritten, code of loyalty to the specifics of Freud's concepts – Freud was the mastermind who was always the final authority on what was psychoanalytic and what was not. He himself analysed most of the first analysts, and they had close, admiring relations with him; they treated him as an intellectual and emotional father figure. Psychoanalysis is often described as a psychology that is in thrall to one particular mind: you will see I use the adjectives 'Freudian' and 'psychoanalytic' synonymously throughout this book. Psychoanalysis was a theory indebted to Freud's excavation of his own autobiography – the self-analysis he carries out in *The Interpretation of Dreams*. Freud analysed himself, and then created a family tree of analysts by analysing his fellow doctors and friends, who went on to analyse others. But Freud is at the root of the tree – the father/source from which all other analysts spring.

Through his vexed relations with his friends and colleagues we can see acted out some of the recurring themes of Freud's own theories, especially (something we will come to in Chapter 3) his theory of the Oedipal desire that the (male) child wants to kill the father and take his place. In his 1920 essay *Beyond the Pleasure Principle* Freud discusses people who repeat the same patterns in all their relationships:

> Thus we have come across people all of whose human relationships have the same outcome: such as the benefactor who is abandoned in anger after a time by each of his *protégés*, however much they may otherwise differ from one another, and thus seems doomed to taste all the bitterness of ingratitude; or the man whose friendships all end in betrayal by his friend; or the man who time after time in the course of his life raises someone else into a position of great private or public authority and then, after a certain interval, himself upsets that authority and replaces him with a new one.
>
> (Freud 1920b: 292)

In this passage Freud seems to be describing his own repeated pattern. His closest and most influential intellectual friendships all ended in bitter disappointment for him, beginning with his professional collaborations with Joseph Breuer and Wilhelm Fliess (1858–1928), and continuing through what he saw as his (and psychoanalysis's) betrayal by C.G. Jung (1875–1961). His friendships with Breuer and Fliess broke down over a combination of intellectual and personal disagreements, and Freud was hurt by their discontinuance, especially that of his relationship with Fliess. Freud and his colleagues seem to act out his own theories – Freud lays down the psychoanalytic law, and the rebellious sons disobey it; they come up with ideas of their own that contradict his, and he kicks them out of the fold.

Breaking away from Freudian orthodoxy has been an aspect of psychoanalysis from its inception, and the debate about Freud continues with great vigour today. Psychoanalysis is a theory of intense emotions. In Freud's world of mental life one loves or hates, longs to be enveloped in womb-like comfort or feels murderous rage; one rarely feels passing interest or minor irritation. It seems appropriate that psychoanalysis has also always provoked intense emotional reactions in both its supporters and its detractors. The extremes of emotion on which the theory relies have spilled over into the debates which rage about the relevance and importance of Freudian ideas today.

Although psychoanalytic discoveries such as the significance of unconscious life, the re-emergence of repressed desires and the centrality of sexuality to our development as human beings have never been superseded, there has recently been a backlash against psychoanalysis as an effective cure for mental illness, and there has been a sustained critique of Freud's historical legacy. On the one hand, Prozac and other antidepressants have opened up a new sense that depression and other mental instabilities can be most effectively treated through drugs. On the other hand, critics of psychoanalysis have pointed out the shakiness of some of Freud's original methods and conclusions.

Both these criticisms – about the new possibilities opened up by drug treatment for explaining and curing mental illnesses chemically, and about the uncertainty surrounding some of Freud's earliest case histories – contain elements of truth, but both are also part of a wider cultural backlash against Freud. (For some particularly virulent anti-Freudians, see the entries on Jeffrey Masson and Frederick Crews in 'Further reading'.) In the final chapter of this book I will return to this question of the relevance of Freud today and argue that it would be a terrible mistake to discard our continued readings of Freud, whether we find ourselves reading with Freud or against him. Many of the conclusions of Freud's detractors are based on their own shaky assumptions. But even if these critiques were 100 per cent true, Freudian concepts would continue to be relevant to any comprehensive understanding of our culture, history and literature, as well as to human mental and emotional life. The reaction against psychoanalysis is part and parcel of the central place Freudian notions have had in our visions of ourselves, our relations with others, and our relation as individuals to our social world.

As we shall see, psychoanalysis is a theory that makes the personal and the theoretical difficult to disentangle. It provides a method for examining the hidden motives that drive even the most apparently objective undertakings, such as scientific endeavours. Psychoanalysis, like Marxism and Darwinism before it, is a theory of the world which casts a sceptical eye on the stories that have preceded it. It suspects stories that come too easily, and asks us to think twice about whether or not we believe that something is true. It is appropriate to turn that psychoanalytic scepticism back on Freud, and to think about his own motivation for constructing his theory, as we continue to explore the basic building blocks of psychoanalytic thought.

KEY IDEAS

EARLY THEORIES

Freud's earliest patients were drawn from Viennese middle-class and upper-class women (and some men as well) suffering from diseases of the nerves. These difficult-to-diagnose diseases, prevalent in both Europe and America at the time, were often connected with, on the one hand, the female sex and, on the other, the stresses of modern urban life. As one British commentator noted of the apparent rise in the level of neurosis, 'the stir in neurotic problems first began with the womankind'; by the 1890s 'daily we see neurotics, neurasthenics, hysterics and the like ... every large city [is] filled with nerve-specialists and their chambers with patients' (Showalter 1985: 121). Neurosis was a slippery category throughout the nineteenth century. Labelling an illness a disease of the nerves often simply meant that a physical cause was not forthcoming.

In 1885 Freud went to study for a short period with the famous French neurologist Jean-Martin Charcot (1825–93) at the Salpêtrière asylum in Paris. By the nineteenth century the Salpêtrière was an asylum for women patients with mental illnesses – mostly hysterics. Interestingly, when the Salpêtrière was originally founded in the late seventeenth century it was a prison for confining prostitutes, 'debauched' girls and female adulterers. An unruly, out-of-control sexuality, and the need to confine or punish that sexuality, link the women prisoners of the seventeenth century with the hysterical women patients of the nineteenth century, as we shall see when we examine the changes brought about by Freud's ideas of the causes of **hysteria**.

THE QUESTION OF HYSTERIA

Freud's development of psychoanalysis's founding concepts, such as the unconscious (see p. 4) and repression (see p. 21), are intimately connected with his experiences of treating his first hysterical female patients. But what precisely is hysteria?

HYSTERIA

Hysteria's symptoms vary: they can include amnesia, paralysis, unexplained pains, nervous tics, loss of speech, loss of feeling in the limbs, sleepwalking, hallucinations and convulsions. Its diagnoses have changed over the centuries, but some beliefs about hysteria remained firmly lodged in place until the late nineteenth/early twentieth century. The word hysteria comes etymologically from the Greek word for 'womb', *hysteron*. Hysteria was initially known as the disease of the wandering womb, and it was believed that only women suffered from it. References to hysterical illness date as far back as an Egyptian medical papyrus from 1900 BC. From the ancient Egyptians onwards, female anatomy was considered an important factor in hysteria: one cause of hysterical behaviour was believed to be women's mobile uteruses that wandered up their bodies away from their proper resting point. Freud's work helped sever the definition of hysteria from its attachment to female anatomy and redefine it as a psychological disease.

Most late nineteenth-century medical practitioners subscribed to one of two conflicting ideas about the causes of hysteria. Some doctors believed that all hysterics were really just attention-seeking fakers. Other, more sympathetic medical commentators assumed that hysteria did exist but that it was a disease suffered only by women. It was no longer believed to be caused by the unlikely wanderings of the womb, but it was still connected with disturbances in the female reproductive organs.

With his work at the Salpêtrière, Jean-Martin Charcot discarded both of these beliefs about hysteria: through his hypnotic experiments he showed that hysterics were not malingering (faking their illnesses); neither was hysteria specifically related to female biology, since some men also manifested symptoms of hysteria. Yet Charcot finally subscribed to strictly physical explanations for hysteria. He maintained the long-standing belief that hysteria could develop only when there was inherited degeneration of the brain. Freud found these explanations for hysteria unsatisfactory, suggesting that, rather than physical causes, the disease might have psychological origins in sexual disturbances from early childhood. Thus, when compared with earlier theorisers of neurotic illnesses, Freud made a significant change: he moved from biological explanations to narrative explanations, from diseased bodies to diseased memories.

In the 1880s and 1890s, when Freud began practising medicine, hysterical illnesses were seen as inherited degenerative diseases caused by a weak constitution – diseased, alcoholic or syphilitic parents, bad blood. One of the key changes that psychoanalysis made in thinking about mental illness was to shift it from a physical to a psychological model. Freud suggested that people could fall ill because of their past history – a traumatic event which happened under stressful circumstances would then be strategically forgotten because it was too painful to recall. Freud and his colleague Joseph Breuer compiled a series of case histories called *Studies on Hysteria* that they published in 1895, in which they unearthed again and again in their patients these traumatic founding moments of mental illness.

Looking at *Studies on Hysteria* one notices first that all the case histories presented are of women. Freud and Breuer's work, by stressing the life stories these women had to tell, shifted the focus of the search for the causes of hysteria from biological sources to narrative sources: the lives the women led, and the stories they told themselves, and refused to tell themselves, about their lives made them susceptible to diseases of the nerves. Recent historians of nineteenth-century hysteria have seen hysteria as a disease that was inseparable from the social position of women at the time. Hysteria has been viewed as a passive form of resistance to the social expectations that surrounded the nineteenth-century bourgeois woman. In an increasingly industrialised society, the middle-class woman was looked up to as a representative of the purity, order and serenity of an earlier time – the guardian of the home fire, the angel at the hearth. A victim of demands that were seemingly at odds with themselves, the nineteenth-century woman was supposed to be gentle, submissive and naive, while also expected to be strong and skilled in her domestic management – a pillar for men to lean on. Hysteria signalled an unconscious protest against these conflicting expectations as well as against the lack of career and educational opportunities available to women. For instance, in *Studies on Hysteria* Joseph Breuer describes his patient Anna O. as unusually intelligent, with a quick grasp of ideas and penetrating intuition. He points out the limited possibilities of her life, considering her immense potential: 'She possessed a powerful intellect which would have been capable of digesting solid mental pabulum and which stood in need of it – though without receiving it after she had left school … This girl, who was bubbling over with intellectual vitality, led an extremely monotonous existence in her puritanically-minded family' (Freud and Breuer 1895: 73–4).

The hysterical woman was frustrated by the tasks expected of nineteenth-century womanhood. She found herself at odds with an image of the maternal figure who nursed the sick and tended to domestic duties. As Carroll Smith-Rosenberg describes her, the hysterical woman began to see what it was like to have her own way:

> No longer did she devote herself to the needs of others, acting as a self-sacrificing wife, mother or daughter: through her hysteria she could and in fact did force others to assume those functions. Household activities were reoriented to answer the hysterical woman's importunate needs. Children were hushed, rooms darkened, entertaining suspended. Fortunes might be spent on medical bills or for drugs and operations. Worry and concern bowed the husband's shoulders; his home had suddenly become a hospital and he the nurse. Through her illness, the bedridden woman came to dominate her family to an extent that would have been considered inappropriate – indeed, shrewish – in a healthy woman.
>
> (Smith-Rosenberg 1985: 208)

Hysteria was a double-edged sword for the nineteenth-century woman patient; on the one hand, illness promised both freedom and attention that was not usually hers for the asking. On the other hand, it increased her dependence, made her a slave to doctors and cures, and made her suspect as a malingerer.

TALKING AND LISTENING CURE

Freud's and Breuer's attempts to cure hysteria must seem humane to us if we look at them in the context of the treatments that were being recommended for neurotic illness at the time. By the 1890s neurosis was seen as a woman's problem that needed firm-handed cures. The assumption that the patient was, at least in part, faking her illness often dictated the term of the cures for hysteria. Throwing water on patients, slapping patients' faces or stopping their breathing were some of the recommended methods for putting an end to hysterical fits (Showalter 1985: 138). In 1873 the American physician Silas Weir Mitchell developed his 'rest cure' for the treatment of neurasthenia, a slightly less violent version of hysteria. Mitchell's rest cure depended upon isolation from family and friends, immobility, no intellectual stimulation of any kind, and an over-inflated diet in which the patient was expected to gain as much as 50 lb. Regaining health often depended upon the fact that the patient would be so happy when the mind-numbing, bodily debilitating cure was finally over that she would take up the burden of her neglected domestic duties with renewed energy.

From this set of recommended cures Freud's and Breuer's experiments with what eventually became the psychoanalytic method made a radical break. They not only believed that their patients' illnesses were real, they also listened to what they had to say. Psychoanalysis relied on the idea that the material of the cure could come only from the patient him or herself. Instead of looking for physical reasons for why someone had a nervous disease, Freud and Breuer listened to their patients' stories, believing that it was in these stories that a cure would be found. Buried in the unconscious were the associations and connections which could make the patient's past and childhood memories make sense. The psychoanalyst's job, like the archaeologist's (one of Freud's favourite comparisons), was to enable the excavation.

When Charcot began studying hysteria in the Salpêtrière in the 1880s, one of his explicit goals was to make the study of hysteria into a respected scientific endeavour. He brought to his efforts a passion for careful observation and classification, and he diagnosed his patients' symptoms in detail. However, looking at the records from the Salpêtrière (especially the photographic evidence of the hysterics in their various poses), one gets the disturbing sense that Charcot was not terribly interested in curing the women under his care. More interested in classification and study than in therapy, he became famous for his public medical displays in which the patients of the Salpêtrière would perform under hypnosis the symptoms of their diseases – arching their backs, frothing at the mouth, showing an incredible tolerance of pain when pins and needles were stuck into their bodies when they were anaesthetised by hypnotic suggestion. Freud and Breuer used Charcot's discoveries about hysteria but took them out of the medical theatre, into the private space of the consulting room. If Charcot's classifications of hysteria depended upon *looking*, Freud's and Breuer's attempts to cure changed the emphasis to *listening*.

HYPNOSIS AND ITS REJECTION

Freud followed many of Charcot's leads in his analyses of hysteria, but he also broke away from some of his central ideas. Initially, like Charcot, Freud employed hypnosis to get through to the root causes of his patients' illnesses. Charcot used hypnosis as a method of understanding hysterical illness, but he also believed that only hysterics were capable of being hypnotised. Hypnotisability for Charcot was a symptom of mental illness. Charcot's theories were challenged, however, by researchers working with hypnotism in Nancy, France. Through carrying out enormous numbers of hypnotic experiments, the Nancy researchers (including Hippolyte Bernheim (1840–1919) and Ambroise Liébeault (1823–1904)) showed that most people were at least potentially hypnotisable. Eventually the Nancy school's beliefs came to be more generally accepted than Charcot's. It is impossible to say accurately what percentage of people are suggestible enough to be hypnotised, but almost all people have some degree of suggestibility that seems to be unrelated to factors such as intelligence or the potential for mental illness.

In the wake of Charcot's and the Nancy school's discoveries, and following on Joseph Breuer's lead, Freud began working with hypnosis in the treatment of his neurotic patients. Initially he used hypnosis to suggest ideas to patients that could help them overcome their illnesses. For instance if someone was unable to move their arm because of a hysterical paralysis, under hypnosis Freud would tell them that they could. But Freud quickly found that these suggestions rarely had the power to alter patients' state of mind permanently. Instead Freud turned again to his colleague Breuer's experiences with his patient

Anna O., to discover another, more fruitful use of hypnosis. Breuer discovered that he could hypnotise Anna O. into remembering the origins of a specific hysterical symptom. If she could then, still under hypnosis, relive the initial experience along with the emotions she had felt at the time, the symptom would disappear. This method of cure Breuer named the **cathartic method**.

THE CATHARTIC METHOD

Catharsis is a Greek word which means purification through purging. Breuer originally adopted this term from Greek tragedy to describe the psychotherapeutic method in which an upsetting event that has caused a hysterical reaction is re-experienced under hypnosis and thereby purged from the system of the person who relives it.

In *Studies on Hysteria* Freud and Breuer stated categorically that 'Hysterics suffer mainly from reminiscences' (Freud and Breuer 1895: 58). Memory, not physiology, was at issue from now on.

Freud eventually extracted two central points from his and Breuer's work with their patients. One point was that unpleasant or traumatic recollections inevitably returned to haunt the memory of the patient. These unpleasant memories were then **repressed** from the patient's conscious knowledge.

REPRESSION

An operation whereby the subject repels, or confines to the unconscious, a desire that cannot be satisfied because of the requirements of reality or of the conscience (see **super-ego** on p. 45). For instance, in one of Freud's cases in *Studies on Hysteria* (Elizabeth von R.) the patient refused to admit to herself that she was in love with her brother-in-law. When her sister died, an upsetting thought entered her mind: 'Now he is free to marry me.' This unwelcome wish had to be immediately repressed – her conscious mind could not allow it in because of the guilt she immediately felt for thinking it. Because it was repressed from her mind it returned, acted out on her body, as a hysterical symptom (see **symptom** on pp. 27–8).

But it was not just any material that was repressed by the unconscious. After writing *Studies on in Hysteria*, Freud came to believe that there was always a sexual content to the repressed unpleasant memory that led to the hysterical illness. If hysterics suffered from reminiscences, they suffered from a specific type of reminiscence: sexual ones. Perhaps, to be more accurate, they suffered from not reminiscing enough; they fell ill from not being able to consciously recall and work through the trauma or traumas of their past.

THE SEDUCTION THEORY AND ITS REJECTION

Freud discovered that, as his patients spoke to him of their pasts, they all brought up surprisingly similar childhood experiences. In their stories their hysterical illnesses inevitably referred back to a scene of sexual abuse by an older figure, usually the father but sometimes another authority figure, or a brother or sister. Interestingly, these sorts of repressed memories were shared by all his patients. Therefore Freud postulated that premature sexual contact or a traumatic sexual attack must have taken place if hysterical illness developed later in life. Although he later revised these ideas, this became his first fully developed theory of the origins of hysteria and neurosis (Freud 1896), the **seduction theory**.

THE SEDUCTION THEORY

Sometimes also known in psychoanalytic terminology as the 'Real Event', Freud's seduction theory stated that repressed memories of neurotics and hysterics inevitably revealed seduction or molestation by an older figure, usually a parent: most often the father. The traumatic event which happened in childhood, however, would not be recognised as traumatic at the time. Instead a delayed reaction set in – an event later in life, when the child reached puberty, would set off a series of recollections in the child's mind, and this delayed recognition would become a pathogenic or poisonous idea that would cause hysterical symptoms later in life. It's interesting to note that Freud calls the seduction theory, the *seduction* theory, rather than the child-abuse theory or the rape theory. Already implied in the word seduction is the possibility of a willing capitulation.

Seduction is a two-way street, involving the victim's desires as well as the aggressor's. Later, when Freud changes his mind about the meaning of this theory and postulates infantile sexual desires, the question of who seduces whom becomes key (see Gallop 1982).

Freud introduced the seduction theory in his essay 'The Aetiology of Hysteria': 'Whatever case and whatever symptom we take as our point of departure, *in the end we infallibly come to the field of sexual experience*' (Freud 1896: 203). But what, precisely, is the field of sexual experience? When Freud wrote those words, in 1896, he was referring to actual bodily contact, but his ideas about that shortly began to change. As Freud continued his work with his patients he began to doubt the status of that repeated scene he had uncovered of a sexual assault by an adult towards a child. In a letter of 21 September 1897 he wrote to his close friend and scientific colleague Wilhelm Fliess that 'I no longer believe in my *neurotica*' (Masson 1985: 264). This did not mean that he thought they were lying to him – rather, he meant that these events that they recalled as having taken place in reality might have actually taken place in fantasy.

The re-emergence of forgotten memories is a key concept for understanding the development of Freud's early opinions about hysteria. But memory itself was not a self-explanatory concept. Is memory always true? Can it be false? When Freud started doubting the literal truth of the stories told by his patients he changed his theory. He began to believe that infantile sexual *desire* alone might be formative of later neurotic symptoms. The scenes of sexual seduction changed direction – it was now the child who desired the parent, not the parent who seduced the child, and the child's seduction of the parent happened in fantasy, not in reality. Freud's concept of **fantasy** became one of the cornerstones of psychoanalysis.

FANTASY

Also spelled Phantasy when used in technical psychoanalytic terminology, this concept involves an imaginary scene in which the subject who is fantasising is usually the protagonist. It represents the fulfilment of a wish in a distorted way, because consciousness cannot allow that wish to be fulfilled in reality, or even straightforwardly in the mind, because of inhibiting factors (see **repression** on p. 21). Fantasy takes numerous forms in order to distort the wish. Fantasies can occur consciously, as in daydreams or conscious desires, but they also can reveal themselves unconsciously through dreams or in primal fantasies (see Chapter 6).

In 1896–97, at the same time that he was changing his ideas about sexual seduction, Freud was also changing his technique. Hypnotising patients in order to get them to speak was difficult for Freud. First, hypnosis was a hit-or-miss affair. Sometimes the patient was not easily hypnotisable, in which case the doctor who was attempting to hypnotise her was made to feel foolish, to lose his sense of control over the situation. You can see how the sense of the doctor's mastery could be lost if you imagine a doctor saying to a patient as he tries to hypnotise her, 'You are fast asleep,' and the patient replying, 'No I'm not.' Freud himself never felt that he was adept at putting his patients into a hypnotic trance. But hypnotising patients also created another problem. With hypnosis the doctor could never be sure that he had not suggested certain ideas to his patients. Therefore, over time, Freud found himself drawn towards a new method of therapy, **free association**. The importance of free association was that the patient spoke for herself, rather than repeating the ideas of the analyst; she worked through her own material, rather than parroting another's suggestions.

FREE ASSOCIATION

One of the cardinal rules of psychoanalytic practice. The patient promises that in the course of the analysis they will say to the doctor whatever comes into their mind as it occurs to them. It is when the patient and the analyst piece together the patient's chain of associations that they can work together to unlock the patient's problems.

SUMMARY

Freud and Breuer broke with a long tradition of treating hysterical women as either having inherited biological diseases or faking their illnesses. They suggested that a disease such as hysteria could be both psychological and real. Believing that the cure for hysteria might come from the patients themselves,

Freud and Breuer listened to the stories their patients told about their own symptoms in order to come to an understanding of the origins of their hysterical illnesses.

Freud found that the memories his patients uncovered about their childhoods often involved early sexual experiences, often attacks by a father or father figure. What Freud came to call psychoanalysis really developed from two major changes in his beliefs: one in his theory and one in his practice. The theoretical change was from belief in the reality of his patients' stories of early sexual abuse to the belief that these stories were often fantasies. (They weren't *necessarily* fantasies, but they could be. See the last chapter for a discussion of the recent controversy about Freud's disavowal of the seduction theory.) Around the same time he also made a practical change: he shifted from the hypnotic technique, in which the analyst might easily suggest ideas to the patient, to the technique of free association, in which the patient did more of the work of talking-through his or her own story to a sometimes largely silent analyst.

Once Freud's ideas about the centrality of fantasy, the importance of childhood sexuality and the method of free association were in place, psychoanalysis began to take form. From these initial ideas Freud would eventually develop most of his later theories about sexual development and the importance of sexuality to society. In the process of his clinical work with patients, Freud continually developed and refined his theory and technique of analysis. It is important to remember that even these initial cornerstones of psychoanalytic belief did not remain unchanged. Psychoanalysis, as we shall see, was as much about the *process* of uncovering the causes of mental illnesses as it was about a single straightforward cure. For Freud, psychoanalysis was a theory of *process* that was also always *in process*. Therefore I will continue to stress the development, contradictions and ruptures, as well as the coherence, of Freud's primary ideas and writings.

INTERPRETATION

When I set myself the task of bringing to light what human beings keep hidden within them … by what they say and what they show, I thought the task was a harder one than it really is. He that has eyes to see and ears to hear may convince himself that no mortal can keep a secret. If his lips are silent, he chatters with his finger-tips; betrayal oozes out of him at every pore. And thus the task of making conscious the most hidden recesses of the mind is one which is quite possible to accomplish.

(Freud 1905a: 114)

The speaker of this passage could easily be Sherlock Holmes describing his method to an admiring Watson. The authoritative tone of the statement is one of a master detective, secure in his penetrating knowledge. However, the final sentence's reference to the 'hidden recesses of the mind' indicates that it is in fact psychological detective work that is being described; S. Freud, not S. Holmes, is the statement's author. Freud made large claims for himself as a detective of the mind, reading closely and carefully the texts at hand. Like his fictional late nineteenth-century contemporary, Sherlock Holmes, he examined the surface content of people's remarks, and their outward appearances and gestures, to excavate the secrets hidden underneath. Psychoanalytic reasoning suggests that our strongest desires appear in our day-to-day lives, even, and especially, when we try to hide them. Through daily occurrences such as slips of the tongue, mistakes, forgetting names, dreams, etc., we betray ourselves; we give our real thoughts and desires away to the canny observer. The analytic method allows one to interpret the cracks in the deceptive outer surface of consciousness to discover the unconscious motives lurking underneath. It is in this sense that Freud's ideas are as crucially concerned with interpretation as they are with sex.

Detectives are primarily interested in who committed a crime and, perhaps, how it was committed. Sherlock Holmes wants to know a criminal's motive only in so far as discovering *why* something was done can lead to discovering *who* it was that did it. Psychoanalysts, on the other hand, are first and foremost interested in motive – the *why* behind the thoughts that run through our heads, the unconscious reasons that underlie our strange dreams or mental disturbances. For Freud, every mental illness has a motive. The task of the analyst and the patient, working together, is, in the first instance, to uncover that motive. But, we might ask, why would someone want to be sick? What purpose could it serve? Psychoanalysis sees illness as always doing some sort of work for the patient: fulfilling some need or desire. By looking at some of Freud's early writings we can see how this emphasis on the uncovering of motive becomes such a central tenet of psychoanalysis, and we can learn what it means to read psychoanalytically.

SYMPTOMS, DREAMS AND SLIPS OF THE TONGUE: *STUDIES ON HYSTERIA* (1895), *THE INTERPRETATION OF DREAMS* (1900) AND *THE PSYCHOPATHOLOGY OF EVERYDAY LIFE* (1901)

In Freud's and Breuer's fascinating collection of case histories *Studies on Hysteria* this detective-like search for a motive for an illness comes to the forefront. As you will recall, nineteenth-century hysterical patients often displayed severe bodily **symptoms** – convulsions, paralysis, loss of speech, etc.

SYMPTOM

Freud found that the hysterical symptom was a strange but meaningful reaction of the body to an unbearable mental situation. A good example of the formation of symptoms can be found in Breuer's case of Anna O. from the *Studies*. While Breuer was treating Anna O. she developed a mysterious abhorrence of water. She found herself unable to drink a drop, although it was the middle of the summer and she was terribly thirsty. Eventually, under hypnosis, she revealed to her doctor and to herself the initial cause of this symptom. She had once gone into the room of her English lady companion and, much to her disgust, found the woman's dog drinking out of a drinking glass. Once Anna had uncovered the source of this symptom, and expressed her horror at the scene (which she had not expressed when it first happened) she was cured of her hydrophobia; she asked Breuer for some water and drank it easily. As we can see from Anna O.'s experience, the doctor helps the patient uncover the original motive for the illness by stirring up the memories of the patient and getting her to narrate the original event. Eventually a connection is made between the past event and the bodily symptom: a story is constructed that makes sense of the patient's previously incomprehensible reactions. Consciously understanding a symptom can make it disappear.

The symptom in psychoanalysis arises through repression (see p. 21). Symptoms emerge when strong emotional reactions are repressed from the conscious mind into the unconscious. They simultaneously become displaced on to the body. Displacement is also central to Freud's theory of symptoms and dreams. Displacement involves the shifting of an emotional reaction from one part of one's life, or one area of the body, to another. The formation of the hysterical symptom consists of a shift in register from the mind to the body; what the mind cannot accept the body acts out without comprehending it.

As discussed above, Freud and Breuer discovered that helping a patient to remember and relive the painful experiences that created the symptom could make the symptom disappear. The doctor and patient worked together to rid the patient of her **traumatic** memories.

TRAUMA

The Greek word for 'wound'. An event in a person's life which is intense and unable to be assimilated. It creates a psychic upheaval and long-lasting effects. When the mind refuses to consciously recognise a traumatic event, the unconscious represses it. The traumatic memory remains, unworked-through in the unconscious, and the affect, or emotional energy surrounding the event, is dammed up. The traumatic event also creates a strange time structure which Freud refers to as *Nachträglichkeit* (usually translated as 'deferred action'). *Nachträglichkeit* describes a situation that Freud frequently encounters in his case studies in which the determining event of a neurosis can be understood only long after it has happened. For instance, a child experiences a sexual assault before he or she really understands sexuality. Years later another event occurs, not necessarily shocking or sexual, that triggers an understanding of, or flashback to, the first event. There is then the realisation that something traumatic happened.

The assumption of *Studies on Hysteria* is that uncovering a reason behind an illness will instigate a cure. Psychoanalytic theory, in this sense, puts a great deal of weight on the act of interpreting and understanding a symptom, as well as on recalling the first time the symptom appeared and what provoked it. Once a problem is consciously understood, rather than unconsciously acted out, the movement towards getting rid of it can begin. The free associations (see definition on p. 24) of patients gave Freud the material on which he based his interpretations.

One topic that sometimes came up in patients' free associations were their dreams. Naturally enough, dreams from the previous night often cling to people's memories in their daily life. Like neurotic symptoms, Freud found that dreams too could be read. He used the same techniques that he had developed for symptoms to do so. By emphasising their significance, Freud saw himself as returning to a pre-modern perspective on dreams. In the ancient world, dreams were seen as having a meaning; their meanings, however, were viewed as prophetic, predicting future events. By the end of the nineteenth century popular opinion looked upon a predictive aspect to dreams as superstition. Many scientists saw dreams as meaningless – a physiological product of what we ate the day before or how soundly we slept. However, in Freud's opinion the modern world, by presuming that dreams reflected nothing but indigestion or some other purely physical explanation, was too quick to dismiss the important idea that they did indeed contain meanings, even if those meanings referred to a person's past rather than predicting his or her future.

Freud considered *The Interpretation of Dreams* (1900) his most important work, immodestly claiming of it that 'Insight such as this falls to one's lot but once in a lifetime' (Freud 1900: 56). It is no coincidence that 'interpretation' is a key word in the title of this fundamental text of psychoanalysis. *The Interpretation of Dreams* is a difficult book to categorise. It seems to combine several genres of writing – part history of dream interpretation, part catalogue of dreams (dreamt by Freud and others), part instruction book for his new psychoanalytic method of reading, even part autobiography. The index of dreams at the back of the book indicates the spectrum of concerns of this compelling volume. To take simply a few of the topics of Freud's own dreams, one could read about his dreams on 'One-eyed doctor and schoolmaster', 'Uncle with yellow beard' and 'Dissecting my own pelvis'. The nature of dreams, as Freud portrays them, is that they are unruly and uncontainable by the bounds of conscious will or common sense. Freud's own book on dreams, at times, seems to mirror this unruliness. Uncovering the desires of the night is a messy business requiring a flexible imagination.

There are few among us who haven't occasionally had an unusual dream. But how does Freud propose we should interpret them? And why is dream interpretation so significant for psychoanalysis? According to Freud, dreams function like symptoms and can be read in a similar way. Hysterical symptoms, however, were confined to the sick. Since healthy people dreamt as much as people who suffered from mental illness, Freud's dream theory postulated a continuum between the neurotic and the non-neurotic. Freud pointed out this paradox of the dreaming state:

> You should bear in mind that the dreams which we produce at night have, on the one hand, the greatest external similarity and internal kinship with the creations of insanity, and are, on the other hand, compatible with complete health in waking life.

(Freud 1910a: 33)

By focusing on dreams, psychoanalysis broadened its scope: although hysterical symptoms presumably appear only in people who are ill with neurosis or hysteria, dreams happen every night to everyone. Psychoanalytic interventions were no longer confined to those in pathological states. *The Interpretation of Dreams* claimed that Freud's methods of deduction were universally applicable to the 'normal' as well as the 'abnormal', and helped to bridge the gap between the two.

Symptoms and dreams are the first two objects of the probing detective gaze of psychoanalysis: making some sort of sense out of apparent nonsense is its initial goal. Freud claimed:

> The interpretation of dreams is in fact the royal road to a knowledge of the unconscious; it is the securest foundation of psychoanalysis and the field in which every worker must acquire his convictions and seek his training. If I am asked how one can become a psychoanalyst, I reply: 'By studying one's own dreams.'

> (Freud 1910a: 33)

One paradox of psychoanalysis is contained in this statement. On the one hand, Freud claims that studying one's own dreams is the best way to become a psychoanalyst – his book is in a very real sense an autobiographical account of his own state of mind, read through his dreams. But Freud will later claim that one cannot ever analyse oneself fully – there will always be blockages, unconscious impulses and desires which refuse to appear unless they are brought to the surface with the help of another. Self-analysis is both necessary and insufficient for working through the psychoanalytic process. Yet Freud's self-analysis founds psychoanalysis; he relates his writing of *The Interpretation of Dreams* to his confused emotional reaction to the death of his father.

In *The Interpretation of Dreams* Freud painstakingly examines many of his own dreams as well as those of his patients and people he knows. He comes to several conclusions about the status of dreaming and its relation to waking life. Freud suggests that, if we look at the dreams of young children, their meanings are evident. His daughter Anna, at nineteen months old, was sick and consequently forbidden food for a day. 'During the night after this day of starvation she was heard calling out excitedly in her sleep: "Anna Fweud, stwawbewwies, wild stwawbewwies, omblet, pudden!"' (Freud 1900: 209). Obviously Anna was dreaming of the food she had been forbidden. In our sleeping state, Freud suggested, we imaginatively satisfy our unfulfilled desires of the day. Typically, he was not content to suggest that some dreams were wish-fulfilments; rather he claimed that *all* dreams were disguised wish-fulfilments. In the *Interpretation of Dreams* one of his most succinct explanations of the significance of the dream is as follows: '*A dream is a (disguised) fulfilment of a (suppressed or repressed) wish*' (Freud 1900: 244). If your conscious, censorious, moral self will not allow the development of certain wishes, then your desires can be satisfied in a dreamy roundabout state, through the distorted world of the dream. Repressed desires are given a stage to perform on at night.

What does it mean that dreams come in disguised form? The baby Anna Freud's wish was not disguised; clearly she wanted food, and in her dream she gorged herself. But for adults and older children the wishes that are satisfied in dreams are often more troubling than the desire for snacks. They often concern thoughts that are unacceptable to the conscious life of our adult selves – sexual desires directed towards inappropriate objects or violent urges directed towards those closest to us. Freud expanded on his initial theory that dreams were all wish-fulfilments to suggest two things: that dreams also expressed infantile material which had been repressed, and that this material was often sexual in nature: 'Our theory of dreams regards wishes originating in infancy as the indispensable motive force for the formation of dreams' (Freud 1900: 747). Like neurotic symptoms, Freud found that dreams were also expressions of repressed wishes – particularly, although not inevitably, sexual wishes.

Both of Freud's main contentions about dreams – that they are inevitably wish-fulfilments and that they usually deal with childhood sexual material – seem counter-intuitive. We can all probably think of dreams we've had which do not subscribe to either of these principles. Freud, at various times, was forced to deal with objections to his theory. What wishes do nightmares or anxiety dreams fulfil? In *The Interpretation of Dreams* Freud attempts to circumvent these objections by finding a wish in every dream – even when a patient dreams something obviously unpleasant to her, Freud imagines that the patient wants to prove him wrong, ergo she's fulfilling a wish. Later in his career, particularly in *Beyond the Pleasure Principle* (1920) (see Chapter 5), Freud was troubled by the existence of certain obviously unpleasant dreams, but generally he stuck to his initial statement, claiming that a comprehensive analysis of a dream will always find the wish hidden behind it.

In a book which followed shortly on *The Interpretation of Dreams*, *The Psychopathology of Everyday Life* (published in 1901), Freud extended his new reading practices further into the mundane daily world. If dreams and symptoms could be read as expressing hidden desires and wishes, so could our mistakes and mishaps.

Examples of parapraxes are easy to find, and Freud's book is full of them. Freud tells the story of the President of the lower House of the Austrian Parliament who declared Parliament closed instead of open at the beginning of a sitting – obviously he was ready for another holiday. The wishes behind parapraxes are often less distorted than the wishes one finds in dreams. When Freudian slips happen they usually provoke smiles in everyone who hears them and recognises their not particularly well hidden meaning. An appropriate one occurred at a psychoanalytic conference: the final contributor, who was closing the conference, addressed the audience by saying 'I'd like to spank the speakers,' instead of thanking them. To an audience of psychoanalysts, a little hostility mixed in with the thanks would come as no surprise.

Parapraxes, dreams and symptoms all express wishes, according to Freud's theories, but these wishes have to be separated into their individual elements before they can be understood. The analytic process of dream interpretation, and the tools which make this interpretation possible, are the best places to look to understand the ramifications of psychoanalytic theories of reading. I will turn now to this important question of the process of making sense in psychoanalysis.

THE TOOLS OF PSYCHOANALYTIC INTERPRETATION: FREE ASSOCIATION, DREAM-WORK, TRANSFERENCE

Is there such a thing as a comprehensive psychoanalytic analysis of a dream? In Freud's theory the interpretation of the dream itself, the actual process of reading the dream, is also always subject to more interpretation. The patient relates her dream to the analyst and then proceeds to free-associate about what recent events, what words, what memories, the dream reminds her of. This process of retelling the dream and discovering what associations the dream brings up uncovers what Freud calls the dream-work, the process by which the thoughts and desires that lie behind a dream become translated, so to speak, into the surface content of the dream (see Wollheim 1971: 69–72). The dream-work can be understood only by seeing the relation between the two different kinds of content that dreams contain – the manifest content and the latent content.

The manifest content of the dream is that which we experience or remember, what the dreams appear initially to be about; the latent content of the dream is its hidden meaning – the repressed unconscious wish or infantile desire. Like symptoms, dreams come in distorted forms; when we dream we have already translated one form of unacceptable desire into another form of potentially obscure or illegible meaning. In order to protect ourselves from the content of our own thoughts we make those thoughts difficult to interpret. According to Freud, only through a process of psychoanalytic interpretation can we reconstitute the latent meaning of the dream from the manifest content.

All dreams are subject to unconscious distortion: that is, the process by which the latent content is transformed into the manifest content. Distortion may give the dream a nonsensical or absurd form, but it won't make one feel guilty or ashamed, the way the undisguised dream-wish might. Condensation is another dream process which contributes to the dream's final form. Freud noticed that 'the manifest dream has a smaller content than the latent one' (Freud 1916–17: 205). In other words, the unconscious material of the dream is condensed, so that each element of the dream we remember represents more than one thought or desire. All the latent dream-thoughts are squeezed into the overdetermined symbolic elements that we remember in the morning.

Overdetermination suggests that each element of the dream contains several wishes and desires which go towards constituting its final form. Therefore, the dream will have different possible interpretations or extractable meanings:

> It is with greatest difficulty that the beginner in the business of interpreting dreams can be persuaded that his task is not at an end when he has a

> complete interpretation in his hands – an interpretation which makes sense, is coherent and throws light upon every element of the dream's content. For the same dream may perhaps have another interpretation as well, an 'over-interpretation', which has escaped him.
>
> (Freud 1900: 669)

Dreams may express several wishes, contain several meanings. An initial reading may always be supplemented by another, by further information or associations.

If one considers the fact that visual and verbal meanings both come into the interpretation of dreams, the ramifications of over-determination become clearer. A simple example may help here. My friend Talia broke her arm and dreamt that she was Napoleon. Napoleon carried his arm the way one does when it is broken, tucked into his jacket as if it were in a sling; yet he was also a powerful leader. One might interpret the wish underlying the dream as a desire to be as powerful as Napoleon, even with a broken arm. But when Talia repeated her dream to another friend he said, 'Of course – Bone-apart!' The dream's meaning emerged through both its visual imagery – the picture of Napoleon Bonaparte with his hand in his jacket – and a punning commentary on the language of his name. Most dreams, of course, are not quite so tidy to interpret, but the combination of words and images that this dream manifests is one of the strongest contributions of Freudian dream interpretation. This simple dream was overdetermined in the context of that combination; the content of the dream could be interpreted both through a visual picture and a linguistic pun. The translations of desires into nonsensical dreams (through the dream-work) and nonsensical dreams back into sense (through narrating the dream and free associations) can be seen as mirror processes. Both work with interpretative abundance, the pos-sibility of many layers of meaning first to disguise and then to uncover.

The meanings of dreams are retrievable only through examining the way in which the patient retells the dream. By putting the dream into language and free-associating around the dream, the patient and the analyst together can construct a better understanding of the dream, the chain of thought towards which it leads, and the memories to which it refers. With the analyst, the patient works through the var-ious associations that the dream brings up. In the interpretation of a dream the patient's associations, and the form and order they appear in, are as important as the actual content of the dream itself. One of the most significant aspects of Freud's interpretative methods is his belief that the process of retelling the dream, the details that are remembered, what is left out on first telling, what is constructed in the process of telling, is as important as the dream itself. In fact there is really no such object as the dream itself without its subsequent account, for we can have no access to dreams except through their subsequent narration. One might suspect that the more a dream is narrated, the more new interpretations might emerge.

Freud's theory of dreams can be seen as containing contradictory elements. On the one hand, I have been stressing the open-endedness of dream interpretation. The meaning of a dream is formulated and reformulated in the act of describing it; new desires, new associations emerge in its retelling. On the other hand, Freud does talk about the 'comprehensive' reading of a dream; in his case histories you will see he often feels that he and his patient have exhausted the possible meanings of a dream and reached a conclusion. Freud also can employ an apparently universal sexual symbolism (although it is important to remember that this symbolism is neither central nor necessary to his theory of dreams as it is laid out in *The Interpretation of Dreams*). One popular image of Freud appears in what is often known as Freudian symbolism, i.e. if you dream about a long or penetrating object such as a snake, knife or sword, the symbol refers to a penis; if you dream about a receptacle such as a jewel box, cave or pocket, the symbol is vaginal. Freud occasionally employs this symbolism in his interpretations, but his theory of dream interpretation is actually at odds with these crude, reductive usages. Freud's theory insists that dreams must be interpreted in the complicated context of each individual telling; their meanings spiral outward, rather then settling so easily on a simple equation, i.e. knife = penis. However, Freud's practice does not always agree with his theory. When his patient Dora describes a dream that included a jewel case belonging to her mother, Freud insists on its vaginal symbolism, later adding: 'The box ... like the reticule and the jewel-case, was once again only a substitute for the shell of Venus, for the female genitals' (Freud 1905a: 114). That 'once again' suggests we are on familiar ground. In an example such as this one, the possibility of meanings multiplying from dreams is denied; one single definitive (and sexual) meaning is substituted.

For psychoanalysis, then, interpretation is a contradictory creature. Freudian symbolism suggests fixed meanings, while Freud's method suggests the limitless possibilities of reading, retelling and constructing the past to fit with, and help, the present. Since the causes of the hysterical symptom are hidden in the patient's unconscious memory, the task of psychoanalysis is primarily that of excavating the patient's past to provide a cure in the present. Remember the central claim of *Studies on Hysteria*: '*Hysterics suffer mainly from reminiscences.*' But, as we have seen, these reminiscences have to be interpreted and understood through the telling of stories in analysis. Initially through his use of hypnosis, Freud found that his patients could remember events and thoughts that were otherwise inaccessible. However, as we discovered in the last chapter, hypnosis was not always successful. Freud soon switched to the method of free association (p. 24), insisting that his patients obey the one cardinal rule of analysis and say everything that came into their head.

Patients didn't always obey this rule, however. Freud found that some of the most significant moments in an analysis were the ones in which the patient couldn't think of anything at all. Silence could indicate that there was some painful memory or thought too close to the surface that needed to be repressed by drawing a blank. But there was another possibility as well. Freud discovered that when patients lapsed into silence it was often because they were having hostile or intimate thoughts about their therapist, and they were embarrassed to tell him what they were really thinking.

These discoveries about the patient's fantasised relations to the doctor were actually of old standing. Breuer's treatment of Anna O. had ended disturbingly for him when, under the influence of hypnosis, Anna declared that she was having Breuer's baby. A shocked and dismayed Breuer promptly abandoned therapy, and never recovered his desire to continue with the kinds of therapeutic methods of *Studies on Hysteria*. Later Breuer refused to support Freud in his contentions that at the base of hysterical illnesses were problems of sexuality. (This is, of course, Freud's version of the story. Critics of Freud have questioned its accuracy.)

Freud similarly discovered that hypnosis could lead to some embarrassing moments. Once, when under hypnosis, a woman patient of his suddenly threw her arms around him (Freud 1925a: 210). These incidents led Freud to think about the way in which an erotic attachment to a doctor might develop in a treatment situation. On the one hand, the incident pointed towards the inevitable sexual element in hysterical illnesses. But it also pointed towards a new idea — what if the doctor was really standing in for an earlier object of love or hate? What if the patient was, in therapy, acting out other relations? This idea became known as **transference**, and became key to Freud's development of the psychoanalytic method.

TRANSFERENCE

Transference suggested that strong emotional, and particularly sexual, feelings — feelings of passionate love and hatred which were originally directed towards others — are transferred on to the doctor in the course of analysis. Initially this seemed like a problem for an analysis — hating or loving the doctor looks as if it would inevitably get in the way of the patient working out their cure. But Freud soon found that transference was a key tool for psychoanalysis. Patients acted out childhood emotions through the relationship with the analyst, initially not realising that they were imitating old patterns. Later they came to analyse and work through these reactions towards the analyst. Ideally they learned to re-attach them to the original figures who inspired the feelings (often their parents). In psychoanalysis 'all the patients' motives, including hostile ones, are aroused; they are then turned to account for the purposes of the analysis by being made conscious, and in this way the transference is constantly being destroyed. Transference, which seems ordained to be the greatest obstacle to psychoanalysis, becomes its most powerful ally, if its presence can be detected each time and explained to the patient' (Freud 1905a: 159). In fact, without transference, analysis cannot properly happen.

Counter-transference was a related development of Freud's theory, pointing out that analysts also had unconscious feelings towards patients, of which they were not entirely in control. Patients might also remind analysts of people from their past, such as their mothers or fathers. Transference and counter-transference are theories of emotional substitution. Behind every initial erotic attachment stands a whole history of previous erotic attachments — each new love (or hate) acts out, rewrites, revises and replays a person's old loves (or hates). Again we can see the importance of the intervention of reading into this unconscious play-acting. If the patient and analyst were to be permanently caught up in the transference, they would be acting like lovers, or child and parent, rather then two people working together to solve a problem. They would be living out emotional dramas, rather than standing back and analysing where those emotional dramas emerged from.

One of the most important contributions of psychoanalysis to a theory of reading is the discovery of this inevitable excess of emotion that accompanies any attempted act of analysis. Sometimes it is very difficult indeed to know if one is through the transference and out the other side. Sometimes it seems that this may be an impossible goal – that every act of interpretation involves the person who is making that interpretation bringing their own emotional baggage into the equation. Psychoanalysis, for all Freud's occasional attempts to insist upon its scientificity as a set of objective theories and methods, in fact calls into question the possibility of anyone standing somewhere totally objective. Transference implies that the *content* of the analysis – the uncovering of early sexual fantasies – may not be as central to the cure as the *process* of analysis – the uncovering, interpretation and working through of these crucial emotional substitutions.

SUMMARY

Freud developed his psychoanalytic method of reading his patients' dreams, speech, emotional reactions and bodily symptoms by interpreting the free associations of his patients. He listened closely to the significance of their silences as well as their talk, their repressions as well as their expressions. For the detective-like Freud, everything about a person was interpretable – everything signified something, every thought that the patient expressed or found himself unable to express was grist to the psychoanalytic mill. The substitution theory of transference indicates that these acts of interpretation always work in two directions, back and forth, between the patient and the doctor. In the transferential situation the analytic session begins to look like a theatre, consisting of many people substituting for various parts at different times. The interpretations of patients' thoughts were connected with the patient's mental state at the moment, but Freud found they were also always related to childhood desires and emotions – the complicated realm of sexuality, to which I will now turn.

3

SEXUALITY

Few of the findings of psychoanalysis have met with such universal contradiction or have aroused such an outburst of indignation as the assertion that
the sexual function starts at the beginning of life and reveals its presence by
important signs even in childhood. And yet no other findings of analysis can be
demonstrated so easily and so completely.

(Freud 1925a: 216–17)

Of all his controversial theories, Freud believed, the one which most
outraged society was his insistence upon the sexual nature of the
child. The writers of the late eighteenth-century Romantic period
helped forge the notion of the child as innocent, a blank slate waiting
to be written on by experience. In contrast, Freud proposed that
childhood fantasies formed a continuum with sexual desires, and
that all children had an innate curiosity about sex and about their
own origins. In the last chapter we looked at how Freud interpreted
neurotic and hysterical symptoms as acting out repressed desires,
and how he saw dreaming as a way of fulfilling these desires
through the unconscious imagination. But what is the content of these
desires? What is it about sexual desires that makes it necessary for
them to be repressed? In this chapter we will explore the centrality of that dangerous topic, sexuality, to psychoanalysis and chart
the ways in which Freud imagines that the spontaneous and far-

reaching desires of infancy become the neurotic and repressed desires of adulthood.

INFANTILE SEXUALITY AND THE OEDIPUS COMPLEX

According to Freud our libido – our basic, instinctual sex drive – leads us towards a build-up of energetic excitation and a subsequent desire for release. (See Chapter 5 for more on this idea.) Freud believed that each infant begins life in a state of polymorphous perversity, loving, eroticising, wanting everything and everyone who interests it. A baby wants to put everything in its mouth, to make everything outside itself a part of itself and its immediate world. The youngest children do not distinguish between the outside world and the boundaries of their own bodies. For the child, becoming aware of oneself as a separate individual is a process of learning to detach an understanding of an interior self from the outer circumstances the world provides. Romantic poets such as William Wordsworth (1770–1850) have also explored this early development of a sense of self, first in an imagined harmony with a maternal body, then forced to separate off into a potentially hostile world. In his long autobiographical poem of 1805, *The Prelude*, Wordsworth describes the happy infant at the mother's breast: 'No outcast he, bewilder'd and depress'd;/Along his infant veins are interfus'd/The gravitation and the filial bond/Of nature, that connect him with the world' (Wordsworth 1970: 27).

As we discussed in the last chapter, Freud's theory of dreams suggested that dreams fulfilled unconscious (or conscious) wishes. At least in our dreams, if not in reality, we can all get what we want. As adults do in dreams, the youngest infants do in real life – they imagine that the world will satisfy their desires instantly. Freud argues that the youngest babies make no distinction between having a desire and fulfilling it – this sort of distinction is something which must be learned. The child at the breast is the best example of this. Until the child finds himself hungry or alone – suddenly not having all his needs met as soon as he has them – he does not conceive of himself as a being separate from the mother (or the breast), whom he sees as an extension of himself. We don't see ourselves as separate from the outside world until the first moment the world doesn't give us what we want. We recognise our separateness, our individuality, at the same time that we discover that our desires aren't always met – that we are beings who can lack something. At the moment we realise that the world around us doesn't always respond to our wishes, we express ourselves by crying out and trying to signal our desires. We learn how to communicate in order to let the world know that something is missing from our lives, that we need more than we are getting.

This moment, which combines the onset of the baby's need to communicate and its sense of a loss of plenitude or oneness with the world, is associated with those early important relations to the parents, who are the first suppliers and withholders of the baby's demands, and the baby's first audience. Freud postulated that one of the primary wishes of early childhood is to be the centre of attention and love from the parents. We can picture this by looking at what Freud imagines happening with the happy, satisfied child nursing at the breast. Sucking at the breast is the first form of infantile erotic satisfaction that Freud identifies. Nursing, of course, is initially for nourishment, for the sake of self-preservation. But one of the key moves that psychoanalysis identifies is from the self-preservative instincts to the pleasure principle (see definition, pp. 82–3), the idea that the primary aim of life is to get as much pleasure as possible: 'The baby's obstinate persistence in sucking gives evidence at an early stage of a need for satisfaction which, though it originates from and is instigated by the taking of nourishment, nevertheless strives to obtain pleasure independently of nourishment and for that reason may and should be termed *sexual*' (Freud 1938: 385). The child will keep sucking even after all the milk is gone – perhaps the child reminds himself that he is protected and loved by the presence of the mother's breast. But there is also, according to Freud, an element of pleasure in this scene of oral satisfaction – an excess beyond what is needed (food) to what is desired (the sensuous enjoyment of the breast). The parents always signify more than just the providers of nourishment and protection to the child – it is in this excess of meaning that what Freud calls sexuality takes hold. In a discussion of thumb-sucking Freud points out that the satisfied baby at the breast prefigures post-coital bliss: 'No one who has seen a baby sinking back satiated from the breast and falling asleep with flushed cheeks and a blissful smile can escape the reflection that this picture persists as a prototype of the expression of sexual satisfaction in later life' (Freud 1905b: 98).

Unfortunately for the self-centred baby, parents are not exclusively focused on the child; they are also interested in each other. The infant, who has, up until the moment of this upsetting realisation, imagined him or herself the centre of the universe, suddenly finds himself relegated to a position of minor importance. The desolate child encounters a new crisis of sexual desire and jealousy that Freud names the Oedipal crisis. Taking the Greek mythical figure Oedipus as a model, Freud claims that typically the child will develop an erotic love for the parent of the opposite sex and a rivalrous hatred for the parent of the same sex who seems to monopolise the other, desired parent. Freud finds a symbolic enactment of his theories of early childhood sexual development in Sophocles' fifth-century BC tragedy *Oedipus the King*. Looking at his development of the Oedipal complex can help us understand the ways in which Freud's ideas about interpretation in analysis overlap with his theories of sexuality. Freud's use of Oedipus is one example of a place where psychoanalytic theory develops from a sophisticated reading of a literary text.

Sophocles' *Oedipus the King* has often been described as the first detective story in the Western tradition. It is a play about uncovering a mystery – or, really, several mysteries. Oedipus, King of Thebes, begins the play by determining to find and eradicate the cause of the pollution in his city that is killing his crops and people. To find the source of the pollution and save the city, an oracle tells him, he must discover who killed the last king, Laius, whose murder has gone unsolved and unpunished. At the beginning of the play Oedipus appears to be an assured and powerful leader; he assumed his crown by solving the riddle of the Sphinx, the exotic, lion-headed beast which had kept Thebes under its spell. By solving the riddle of the Sphinx he freed the city from enslavement. He then married Laius's widow, Jocasta, and became king himself. The confident Oedipus initially pictures himself as a master reader, an expert at solving puzzles; he is one who uncovers truth and leads the way to knowledge. During the course of the play Oedipus discovers that he himself is the criminal whom he seeks; he murdered Laius unknowingly in a fight before he first arrived in Thebes. But, worse, Oedipus also discovers that Laius and Jocasta were his parents, who abandoned him as a child because of a prophecy which warned them that their son would kill his father and marry his mother. Through no fault of his own Oedipus is the source of the poison in the city. It is the riddle of his own birth – his unknowing murder of his father and incestuous marriage to his mother – that has brought the gods' curse upon his city. He is the answer for which he seeks: specifically his mysterious (murderous and incestuous) origins are what is at issue. At the end of the play Jocasta hangs herself, and Oedipus blinds himself so that he will no longer have to see the results of his incest and murder.

Freud found in the myth of Oedipus a version of a tragedy that he saw as enacted in every family, although on a less dramatic scale. Oedipus, according to Freud, acted out a wish that everyone has in early childhood. In his clinical work, and, significantly, in his own self-analysis, Freud continuously found this recurring pattern – of attraction to and love for the parent of the opposite sex, and jealousy and hatred, even a death wish, towards the parent of the same sex – that he eventually named the Oedipus complex. In *The Interpretation of Dreams* (1900) Freud claims that *Oedipus the King*'s continuing power over a modern audience is because of the recognition we all have of the story of the play from our earliest childhood. According to Freud, we recognise that Oedipus's strange, incestuous destiny might have been our own:

It is the fate of all of us, perhaps, to direct our first sexual impulses towards our mother and our first hatred and murderous wish against our father. Our dreams convince us that this is so.

(Freud 1900: 364)

Note that Freud's phrase 'all of us' brings up a problem about who the Oedipus complex describes. Are 'all of us' men? Throughout this chapter I have been using the masculine pronoun to refer to the infant of psychoanalytic theory, because Freud himself assumes a generic male child. But if Freud's 'all of us' refers to boys *and* girls, and if we imagine that the closest thing to a universal experience of childhood is that blissful picture of the baby at the breast, then all babies – boys and girls – should learn to love their mothers first and most intensely. Logically, everyone should direct their first love towards their mother and see their father as an unwanted intruder into that relationship. To keep his stories symmetrical, and to keep heterosexuality as the normal standard of healthy sexuality, Freud has to reverse this story for girls. He reconstructs the primary object of the young girl's desire as her father, and the object of her hatred as her mother. I will return to the complicated ways in which Freud manoeuvres the Oedipus complex in order to explain female sexuality. For the moment let us just note that Freud's Oedipus complex is designed with the baby boy in mind. Although this is a problematic assumption, one with which many feminist critics have disputed, at this point I will continue with Freud's fiction that the 'typical' child is male and describe his theories about what happens to the baby boy during the course of the Oedipus complex.

During the Oedipal stage the baby focuses all his attention on his mother and wants to have her all to himself. Soon, however, he realises that there is someone else, the father, in competition for his mother's love. He begins to develop rivalrous and antagonistic feelings towards his father when he sees that his mother's attention is also directed towards this other person. The baby wishes the father out of the way. In his young mind he becomes a baby murderer: he imagines killing the father so he can take his place. Sadly the violent young lover, at this point, must learn that he can't always get what he wants. The father, who is much more powerful than the baby, threatens to punish the child if the child doesn't stop coveting the mother. The best the baby boy can hope for is to grow up to be *like* his father and eventually find someone *like* his mother. The child thus identifies with the father or takes him for a role model. In the Freudian schema, when the baby settles for identifying with his father, rather than wanting to kill him, he also internalises the threatening, punishing aspect of the father.

THE SUPER-EGO

This fear of the father's power becomes the baby's super-ego, the internal voice which stops the child from doing things he shouldn't do, or makes him feel guilty for having done things he shouldn't have done when he does do them. (See Chapter 5 for a more detailed look at the super-ego.)

Freud's story of Oedipus, in a sense, bridges the gap between issues about interpretation that I discussed in the last chapter and the issues about sexuality that I am introducing here. In the dreams of his patients and himself, Freud found stories about people's pasts which he decoded using his therapeutic method of free association. By understanding the processes of displacement, overdetermination and condensation which gave the dream its manifest form, Freud traced back the information that went into the dream and constructed the latent meaning of the dream, the wish that was fulfilled in it, the childhood material to which it referred, and the daily residues (or recent happenings) that contributed to its final form. In the course of describing these processes in *The Interpretation of Dreams* Freud came upon a factor that he saw as an inevitable early-childhood source of dreams and neurosis – the crisis of desire around the feelings of love and hatred towards the parents. According to Freud, the negotiation of the Oedipal complex as a child is an integral part of everyone's sexual development, whether that development is healthy or neurotic.

Freud's initial working out of the Oedipus complex takes place in the light of his own self-analysis and issues around his father's death, which happened while he was beginning work on *The Interpretation of Dreams*. Freud saw the same dynamics of love and jealousy in himself as a child as he found in his neurotic and hysterical patients. He wrote in a letter of 15 October 1897 to his friend Wilhelm Fliess:

> A single idea of general value dawned on me. I have found, in my own case too, [the phenomenon of] being in love with my mother and jealous of my father, and I now consider it a universal event in early childhood … If this is so, we can understand the gripping power of *Oedipus Rex* … The Greek legend seizes upon a compulsion which everyone recognises because he senses its existence within himself.
>
> (Masson 1985: 272)

The myth of Oedipus is a story about coming to painful self-knowledge, the same sort of self-awareness that Freud enacts when he talks about his recognition of Oedipus within himself. Freud sees in Oedipus a mirror image of himself, a confident leader who solves one riddle of humanity, only to be brought down by another – the tragic story of his own origins, a story over which he has no control.

The Sphinx initially asked Oedipus a riddle: what walks on four legs in the morning, two legs in the afternoon and three legs at night? The answer, which Oedipus alone was able to decipher, was mankind: man crawls on all fours as a baby, walks upright as an adult, and leans on a cane as an aged person. In this mythical riddle Freud sees an allegory of the child's desire for knowledge about the origin of babies which is 'the oldest and most burning question that confronts immature humanity' (Freud 1907b: 177). Freud suggests that children, seeking answers to these questions about their own origins, are like Oedipus, who thinks he knows all the answers but misses the fact that he does not know the secret of his own obscure and cursed beginnings. The child's love for the mother and envy and hatred of the father are enacted over and over again in these early dramas.

According to psychoanalysis, there is no escaping those first primitive desires and instincts. But psychoanalysis also suggests that the process of fully understanding these desires is one about which we should never be too confident. Oedipus's misplaced confidence acts as a warning to the analyst who thinks he has unlocked the secrets of the unconscious. I am suggesting that there are two different versions of Freud that come through in his fascination with Oedipus. The first is the confident, Sherlock Holmes-like Freud, who thinks he can uncover all the secrets of the unconscious. That Freud sounds like the Oedipus who is sure of what he's looking for. But, as we know, that Oedipus was mistaken. He was not as good a reader as he thought he was. The other Freud recognises that knowledge is always partial and subject to blind spots; he sees that we cannot separate our emotional attachments from our knowledge of the world – that there is no such thing as an absolutely objective perspective on ourselves. That Freud sees that passionate transferences of childhood emotions affect every relation to knowledge. At the end of Sophocles' play, when Oedipus blinds himself, he does so in part because he discovers that he was already blind: blind to his own guilty desires. Self-knowledge, for Freud the end-goal of interpretation, turns out to hinge on the realm of sexuality – uncovering the early frustrated passions for the first and most important figures in the baby's early life, the parents.

THREE ESSAYS ON THE THEORY OF SEXUALITY (1905)

Throughout the earlier part of his career Freud, perhaps surprisingly, managed to make the differences between male and female unimportant to his theory of sexuality. In the psychoanalytic theory of infantile sexuality there is no real distinction between what girls and boys want – these distinctions do not develop properly until puberty. What is important, however, is the difference between what Freud calls the masculine or active principle and the feminine or passive principle.

Freud assumes that all libido – all sexual drive – is fundamentally active, and therefore masculine. But Freud also found that young children, in the process of discovering their sexuality, took up different positions at different times – sometimes they imagined themselves as active, and sometimes they imagined themselves as passive. Femininity and masculinity were seen as movable positions rather than fixed identities. Each man or woman had aspects of their personality that were masculine and feminine.

Freud's ground-breaking articles, the *Three Essays on the Theory of Sexuality* of 1905, expand on these concepts of activity and passivity to open up a host of possible positions for the desiring infant. In the *Three Essays* sexual desire is not so much structured along bisexual lines – a struggle between masculine and feminine, or active and passive desires – as structured by *polysexuality* – the possibility of having varied desires and objects of those desires. In the *Three Essays* Freud distinguishes between the sexual object (the person or thing who is the object of sexual attachment) and the sexual aim (the sexual activity one imagines involving that person or thing). He suggested that the sexual object and the sexual aim are only loosely and contingently bound together – we can see this by looking at the free-ranging sexuality of young children. There is no natural, biological law which guarantees that desire will be heterosexual and procreative. Instead, sexual development is a process of multiple desires becoming disciplined and, in a sense, narrowed. The Oedipus complex can be seen as the story Freud creates about growing up and taming these radical and multiple desires. If the Oedipus complex is universal, it guarantees that desire is channelled into the one socially acceptable direction; the boy initially for the mother and then for a (female) substitute for the mother; the girl initially for the father and then for a (male) substitute for the father.

One goal of Freud's sexual theories is to expose the continuities between sexual and non-sexual love, between the love of the child for the parent and the later loves, sexual activities and sexual perversions which recall this relationship. Conversely, Freud also suggests, the love the mother feels for the child can also be seen as continuous with sexual desire:

> A mother's love for the infant she suckles and cares for is something far more profound than her later affection for the growing child. It is in the nature of a completely satisfying love-relation, which not only fulfils every mental wish but also every physical need; and if it represents one of the forms of attainable human happiness, that is in no little measure due to the possibility it offers of

satisfying, without reproach, wishful impulses which have long been repressed and which must be called perverse. In the happiest young marriage the father is aware that the baby, especially if he is a baby son, has become his rival, and this is the starting-point of an antagonism towards the favourite which is deeply rooted in the unconscious.

(Freud 1910b: 209–10)

Desire and rivalry flow both ways in Freud – from children to parents, but also from parents to children. Psychoanalysis suggests that we never really grow up, we never completely leave those childhood urges behind. They exist in the unconscious and return to haunt us in neurotic illnesses, in dreams, in our various sexual preferences.

Freud's repeated conclusions in *Three Essays on Sexuality* is that the developmental narrative he tells, and its movement towards adult 'normal' sexuality, is a very difficult path for the child to negotiate successfully. Because children enter the world as polymorphously perverse creatures, having drives, needs and wants which can be satisfied and frustrated in a huge variety of ways, it is difficult to see how all these multitudinous desires inevitably get channelled in the same narrow direction – towards adult procreative heterosexuality. The very definition of normal becomes shaky in the *Three Essays* because the perverse, that which swerves from the norm, is no less likely to happen than anything else. Reading the *Three Essays* one begins to see why Freud's complicated 'normal' narrative of developing sexuality through the proper stages of the Oedipus complex is rarely achieved. Who you love, who you hate, who you fear and who you identify with as a child switches around – it is not written in stone.

The *Three Essays on the Theory of Sexuality*, along with *The Interpretation of Dreams*, contain the bedrock of Freud's theories. These were the two books he updated constantly during his lifetime. They outline his theory of neurosis and explore the crucial area of libidinal drives. The *Three Essays* cover the sexual aberrations, infantile sexuality and puberty.

PERVERSIONS

Freud begins with the idea of the sexual perversions as pathological, and proceeds to confront his readers with the reasoning behind all the variety of sexual practices that were then considered abnormal, such as fetishism, homosexuality and voyeurism. Freud defines perversions in the following way: 'Perversions are sexual activities which either (a) *extend*, in an anatomical sense, beyond the regions of the body that are designed for sexual union, or (b) *linger* over the intermediate relations to the sexual object which should normally be traversed rapidly on the path to the final sexual aim' (Freud 1905b: 62). The final sexual aim, in this definition, is genital intercourse; the assumption is that sex is primarily defined by that which leads towards reproduction.

Through his explanations Freud goes on to overturn the conventional societal perspective on perversion, which defined perversion as any form of sexual act which did not lead to copulation. He pointed out that the goals of pleasure and procreation do not coincide – sexuality is much more to us than the guarantor of the reproduction of the human race. The human reproductive function is, in a sense, overwhelmed by the emotions we attach to the realm of sex.

In the first section of the *Three Essays on Sexuality*, Freud extended the range of the perversions, to make it impossible not to recognise that every sexual relation included some form of perversion – some form of sexual congress which was not strictly in the service of procreation. Freud describes a kiss in such a way as to point out its essential perversity: 'the kiss, one particular contact of this kind, between the mucous membrane of the lips of the two people concerned, is held in high sexual esteem among many nations (including the most highly civilised ones), in spite of the fact that the parts of the body involved do not form part of the sexual apparatus but constitute the entrance to the digestive tract' (Freud 1905b: 62). Describing a kiss as consisting of contact between mucous membranes, and pointing out its proximity to the digestive tract, exemplifies one of Freud's cleverest rhetorical techniques in the *Three Essays*. By showing the proximity between behaviour that society defines as normal and abnormal sexuality he indicates the multitude of ways in which the two categories can shade into each other.

Freud outlines his three central points about the unstable relation between desire and procreative sexuality in his late explanatory work, *An Outline of Psychoanalysis*:

(a) Sexual life does not begin only at puberty, but starts with plain manifestations soon after birth.

(b) It is necessary to distinguish sharply between the concepts of 'sexual' and 'genital'. The former is the wider concept and includes many activities that have nothing to do with the genitals.

(c) Sexual life includes the function of obtaining pleasure from zones of the body – a function which is subsequently brought into the service of reproduction. The two functions often fail to coincide completely.

(Freud 1938: 383)

Infancy brings with it, from Freud's observation, a fascination with sexuality and the baby's own genitals. This can continue approximately up to the age of five, after which the child enters a period of latency, in which the sexual drive is not as obvious or active, until puberty. The early period of life inevitably falls victim to infantile amnesia – a universal forgetting of everything that happened during our childhood, often up to the age of six or seven. According to Freud, children, like neurotics, repress memories to cover up sexual knowledge. 'Can it be, after all, that infantile amnesia, too, is to be brought into relation with the sexual impulses of childhood?' Freud asks (Freud 1905b: 89). Infantile amnesia, according to Freud, conceals from the child the beginning stages of his own sexual life. Psychoanalysis centrally concerns itself with unearthing these early experiences, emotions and desires. As we saw in the last chapter, psychoanalysis attempts to cure by freeing this repressed knowledge, so that it can be used and understood. Amnesia, which Freud claims accompanies all of us about our early sexual lives, is also found in neurotics who repress and forget things they should know about their own desires. Babies are, in a sense, often healthier than adults, because they act on their erotic wishes rather than repressing and inhibiting them.

Our first infantile erotic satisfactions are oral – the baby early learns to experience the world by putting what he can in his mouth, hoping that whatever it is will give him the same satisfaction that the breast once did. Freud names this erotic hunger for the world the *oral* stage. Much infantile activity, such as thumb-sucking, represents this stage of development, when the child hopes to attain its pleasure from the world by putting everything it can into its mouth.

The next erotogenic zone that the child discovers as he explores his own body is the anus. The *anal* stage emerges from the pleasure the child takes in his excretory functions. Anal pleasure comes initially for the child from emptying his or her bowels; the bowel movement is often viewed (by both parents and child) as the child's first gift to the parents. Anyone who has ever watched parents doggedly pursuing their child's potty training knows the kind of attention every bowel movement can come in for. It is not surprising that what the child takes into his body and what he expels from it become so central to the child's growing image of himself, for these very issues occupy the parents as they watch over the child's growth. The holding back and expulsion are related to issues of control, orderliness and neatness later in life. The anal personality, as we have come to know it in popular jargon, refers to someone who is, according to Freud, 'orderly, parsimonious, and obstinate' (Freud 1908c: 209). If faeces are the child's first gift to the parents, then, later, faeces and money can come to be associated in fantasy life.

The third and final erotic stage of infancy is the *genital* phase – also sometimes called the phallic phase, although it refers to both boys and girls. (It is important to remember that for Freud the three phases tend to emerge in that general order but they always overlap each other – it is not simply that one is replaced by the next.) In the genital phase the baby becomes aware of his genitals as a source of stimulation, exploring his own body in the normal course of events through masturbation. Infants can also be stimulated by being rubbed with a towel or by lots of other everyday occurrences that happen while taking care of a baby. If you remember, Freud initially believed that child abuse was always a key factor in the later development of sexual neurosis. In the seduction theory he stated that a parent or another older authority figure seduced or sexually attacked the inno-cent child, leading to later neurosis and hysteria. By the time he is writing *Three Essays* (1905) this theory has been superseded by the normality of infantile libidinal desires and fantasy. Children may suffer from abuse, and that certainly may lead to later neurotic illness, but children also have erotic desires of their own without any interference from others. The parents are usually the first objects of desire and fantasy for the child, for they are literally the first bodies with whom the child comes into contact.

To recapitulate Freud's major points from the *Three Essays* and his other early works on sexuality: the sexual theory Freud proposed in the first decade of the twentieth century did not distinguish between boys and girls. Both resembled adults in the passionate sexual nature of their attachments; both boys and girls had wider-ranging non-genital sexual lives than adults; both, in the forgotten period of infancy, and later in the revived sexual development of puberty, reacted to the sexually desired (and desiring) parental figures of childhood. Sexual pleasure could arise from any part of the body for infants. Therefore sexuality has to be understood as a term which refers to more than just pleasure received from genital sensation. The 'foreplay' of a kiss or other sexual activity, when viewed in the light of the reductive perspective that claimed that the aim of all sexuality was procreation, was seen as aberrant or perverse. Freud centrally pointed out that sexual instincts did not necessarily simply focus on the genitals. The sexual instincts were divided up into an aim (an activity that would help one achieve pleasure) and an object (the thing or person that will satisfy the aim), and there was no guarantee that aims and objects would correspond in ways that would conform to societal assumptions that suggested that boys should have active sexual aims towards girls, for instance, or that girls should have passive sexual aims towards boys.

Sexual difference, which eventually emerges as a factor in Freud's theory in puberty, begins only then to suggest a 'natural' path for each child's desires to take – girls gravitating towards their father and boys towards their mother. But Freud's central theory of sexual development, the Oedipus complex, was built for boys, not for girls, and for heterosexuals, not homosexuals. Freud's conclusions in the *Three Essays on the Theory of Sexuality* leaves open the possibility that what is defined as 'natural' sexuality is a later societal imposition. Baby boys and baby girls have **ambivalent** attitudes towards both parents.

AMBIVALENCE

Ambivalence is the simultaneous coexistence in the mind of opposite emotions, particularly love and hate. It is a very important emotional state for psychoanalytic theory.

Freud writes:

> a boy has not merely an ambivalent attitude towards his father and an affectionate object-choice towards his mother, but at the same time he also behaves like a girl and displays an affectionate feminine attitude to his father and a corresponding jealousy and hostility towards his mother.

(Freud 1923: 372)

It seems that the heterosexual object choice is no more natural or set than the homosexual one. The interest of Freud's theories is often in his wavering between a normalising sexual development and the radical possibilities that infantile sexual desire is not set in any one path. I will turn in the last section of this chapter to Freud's explanations for how sexuality comes to be policed and heterosexualised, and this will lead us back to the question of what psychoanalysis has to offer as an explanation for the sexual development of the girl child.

CASTRATION AND PENIS ENVY

The third phase of the child's sexual development, the genital stage, involves the child's exploration of its own body and the discovery that masturbation can bring pleasure. This discovery, perhaps more so in Freud's day but still sometimes today, is often accompanied by a parental command to the child prohibiting masturbation and a threat that something terrible may happen if the child continues to indulge in his early sexual explorations. Freud associated this threat with the baby boy's fear of punishment inflicted by the cruel father who interrupts the boy child's happily erotic relationship with its mother. The punishment that the father threatens is castration – the removal of the organ that the child comes to associate with sexual pleasure and desire. When fear of the father makes the child give up his desire to have his mother, he is responding to the **castration complex**.

THE CASTRATION COMPLEX

In Freudian theory the castration complex, the fear of the loss of the penis for boys and the recognition of the loss of the penis for girls, emerges from a number of different sources and affects both boys and girls, although they experience it very differently. As the child grows up he comes to puzzle over the problem of sexual difference. What makes boys and girls two separate categories of people? Freud presumes that at some point there is a visual element to this conundrum. The child sees the genitals of the other sex and realises (if he's a boy) that the other sex is missing something that he has or (if she's a girl) that the other sex has something that she is missing. Both of these recognitions are traumatising, nearly catastrophic.

According to Freud's logic, the boy fears that the girl once had a penis but that it was cut off – he translates this fantasy into anxieties about the continued health and wholeness of his own organ. For the little boy, therefore, the castration complex is a relatively straightforward affair – he associates the loss of his penis as a possible outcome of bad behaviour – reasoning, 'Look, it's already happened to girls; it might happen to me.' He fears and loathes his father, who stands between him and his mother, but finally submits to the father's rule, agreeing to grow up to resemble his father and find a substitute for his mother.

As we have repeatedly seen, Freud's model child going through the Oedipal complex is a boy. How does the little girl give up desiring her mother and begin desiring her father? What if she doesn't give up desiring the mother? These are two of the questions which lurk around the edges of Freud's ongoing problems understanding femininity. He wrote in a letter to the analyst Marie Bonaparte: 'The great question that has never been answered and which I have not yet been able to answer, despite my thirty years of research into the feminine soul, is "Was will das Weib?" ["What does Woman want?"]' (Jones 1955: 468–69). We will return to this question, and Freud's problems in analysing women's sexuality, when, in Chapter 4 on Freud's case histories, we discuss the case of Dora, but for the moment let us try to follow Freud's logic concerning the girl's relationship to castration anxiety.

According to Freud, the girl's sexual development works in a slightly different, and much more convoluted, way. What the girl realises when she sees the genitals of the opposite sex may be seen as much more devastating than what the boy realises. Psychoanalysis argues that she sees her lack of a penis as a sign that she has already been castrated – she has no penis and she wants one. She also realises that her mother (who up to that point has served as her primary love object) has failed her – her mother is similarly penis-less and she certainly can't give the disappointed girl one. Psychoanalytic logic claims that the girl, in anger at her mother, turns to her father, and surmises that if he can't give her a penis he may be able to give her a baby as a substitute. All these assumptions, Freud believes, emerge from the child's imperfect understanding of, and grasping after, sexual knowledge. Boys develop castration anxiety – a fear of losing the penis – but girls develop penis envy – a jealousy about not having a penis.

The story which Freud constructs for the little girl is not an obvious one, and it has provoked heated debate over the years among early analysts and later feminist critics alike. By the late 1910s and 1920s Freud's followers were beginning to argue with him about his theories of sexual difference. The debates about femininity which took place in the 1920s are one of the few times when Freud's ideas were seriously disputed within the psychoanalytic community. Penis envy was a particularly controversial topic. Many analysts felt that Freud's mistake was to assume that the development of the girl simply mirrored that of the boy – that the girl was incapable of having her own separate development. However, analysts who wanted to make the development of the girl completely separate from that of the boy from birth found themselves returning to a type of biological determinism in which anatomy determines an individual's desires. This ran counter to the many aspects of Freud's work which showed that sexuality for humans was much more than biological instinct.

If the story of the girl's uncertain development towards adult heterosexual desire is a problem for Freud, then it is also clear that the fact of adult homosexuals – men and women who desire members of their own sex – is similarly troubling to a strict reading of Freud's Oedipal story. In the late nineteenth century a series of newly formed clinical descriptions began to emerge around homosexuality, which was then seen as deviant behaviour. Those descriptions were predicated upon the fact that heterosexuality was taken to be the norm. (When speaking of this, however, we should proceed cautiously, because it is important to remember that the terms 'heterosexuality' and 'homosexuality' first appear in print only in the 1890s. They are modern, historically constructed categories of how we organise relations between the sexes.) Medical and sexological discussions of homosexuality in the late nineteenth century considered it an innate, congenital condition, in contrast to the popular perception of it as a wilful choice or one religious understanding of it as a sin. Freud's positing of the child as polymorphously perverse led him to view homosexuality as on a continuum with heterosexuality. On the one hand, Freud sees everyone as having homosexual urges and tendencies – the development of the Oedipal complex which sees the boy desiring his mother and the girl desiring her father is rarely pure or straightforward. The strong feelings of love and hate directed towards the parents are potentially shifting and substitutable. On the other hand, Freud also defines homosexuality as a deviation from the norm, and an early stage through which children or adolescents pass on their way to adult heterosexuality. Homosexuality is also, damningly, linked by Freud with narcissism – taking one's own self as a sexual object. (See p. 78 for more on narcissism. Also see pp. 73–75 for Freud's case history 'The Psychogenesis of Homosexuality in a Woman' for more on Freud's understanding of homosexuality.)

So we see that Freud's understanding of femininity and of homosexuality are often interestingly self-contradictory. One of Freud's radical moves was to assume that biology didn't set the grounds for all further development – that the things that happened to one in early childhood and the stories that were told to the child (and that the child told to him or herself) contributed to how one grew up as a sexed human being. For Freud, you might want to argue, women and men were made, not born. The assumption of sex and gender roles was a process which could move in any number of directions, not a biological fact carved into the stone of the body. So, even if some of the stories Freud came to tell about the development of the boy and girl may now seem absurd or untenable, his great discovery was to realise that people's sexuality emerged from the translation of instinctual drives into stories – stories that involved the parents and the young lover's early life, stories that children told to themselves and to each other about where babies came from, fears and anxieties about punishment, and fantasies about love.

SUMMARY

Freud's sexual theories of the first decade of the twentieth century posited polymorphously perverse desiring infants who resemble adults in the passionate sexual nature of their attachments. According to Freud, boys and girls have wider-ranging non-genital sexual lives than adults; in his *Three Essays on Sexuality* (1905) Freud widens the definition of sexuality to encompass more than just pleasure received from genital sensation. The sexual instincts are divided up into an aim (an activity that will help one achieve pleasure) and an object (the thing or person that will satisfy the aim), and there is no guarantee that aims and objects will correspond to their socially acceptable forms. Sexual difference enters Freud's theories only in the later stages of infantile sexuality, with the Oedipus complex. In the forgotten period of infancy, and later in the revived sexual development of puberty, boys and girls react to the sexually desired (and desiring) parental figures by taking their places in the Oedipus complex and negotiating its attached anxieties – for boys, the castration complex; for girls, penis envy. It was through Freud's case histories that he came to advance these strange stories of childhood sexuality, and it is to these tales that we now turn.

4

CASE HISTORIES

Freud's case histories are some of his most accessible and fascinating works. Each unfolds like a psychological mystery, compulsively readable; we follow along with Freud's diagnoses and his various patients' reactions to his interpretations of their symptoms, as they try to puzzle out the contents of their own minds and the causes of their illnesses. Freud developed psychoanalytic theory through his practice of unearthing the stories of his patients' pasts. But his writing up of the case histories into publishable form involved another type of narrative as well – the story of the analysis itself: the uncovering of the material which unravelled the patients' hidden memories. In a sense, each case history of Freud's contains at least two stories: the story of the past events and fantasies which led to the patient's illness and his or her seeking of psychoanalytic help; and the narrative of the analysis with Freud, which, piece by piece, constructs and reconstructs those past experiences. Freud's case histories have been particularly rich sources for literary critics who are interested in exploring the way narrative structure can affect narrative content, and the question of how or if we can securely distinguish between 'history' and 'story' (see Brooks 1985; Bernheimer and Kahane 1985).

Despite the importance of these individual cases to Freud's creation of psychoanalysis, Freud wrote and published very few case histories in his lifetime, all of them towards the beginning of his career. One problem he encountered was that of privacy – the intimate sexual material contained in a case history was potentially recognisable to readers of the inbred intellectual society of turn-of-the-century Vienna, even though Freud always disguised the people he wrote about by giving them false names. Freud's patients were often the wives of his friends or themselves people he knew in other capacities. Because psychoanalytic interpretation of dreams and symptoms often referred to punning meanings of names and places, Freud had to go through convoluted changes in order to try to protect his patients' privacy while still retaining the double meanings of the proper names. This problem of the relation between intimacy and exposure, between what is necessary for the sake of medical accuracy and what is too revealing for the reading public, or the privacy of the individual, to sanction, pervades Freud's writing of his case histories.

Studies on Hysteria is Freud's first foray into the art of the case history. Because, however, the cases in the *Studies* were carried out before the psychoanalytic method was fully developed, when Freud and Breuer were still employing hypnosis and the cathartic method, I have discussed them in Chapter 1 instead of here. After his initial writing-up of his patients' stories for *Studies*, Freud refers to many of his cases in passing (especially in his early books, such as *The Interpretation of Dreams*), but he records only six of them for publication. Two out of those six he did not witness first-hand. One of the second-hand cases is his analysis of the judge Daniel Paul Schreber, who was institutionalised with psychosis. Freud never actually met him but wrote a fascinating analysis of the material Schreber put into his memoir of his own severe mental distress. The Schreber case is therefore a psychoanalytic reading of a text, rather than an analysis of a person. In some ways it has more in common with Freud's readings of other literary and artistic works than it does with the other case histories. Another case history, that of Little Hans, a five-year-old boy with a phobia of horses, was also carried out at a distance. Freud met the child only once; the bulk of the analysis of the child's fear of horses was conducted by the boy's father, who was a follower of Freud's. *Little Hans* is itself a marvellous read – it is obvious that Freud is very fond of his young patient once removed. Hans's fascination and fear about his own genitalia and that of his parents' helped Freud formulate many of his ideas about the castration complex and childhood theories of where babies come from. It is also interesting to note that, despite the fact that Little Hans is brought up by what we would probably call enlightened or liberal parents who are followers of Freud, he is still told by his mother at an early age that if he continues to masturbate the doctor will cut off his penis. It is important to keep in mind the kinds of threats that young children were subject to more regularly in the late nineteenth and early twentieth century, to understand how ideas such as Freud's castration complex might emerge from a repressive social atmosphere around sexuality.

Other than the stories of *Studies on Hysteria*, Freud published only four case histories of people who were actually his patients: 'Dora', who was treated for eleven weeks before she broke off the analysis in 1900; the Rat Man, who was treated in 1907; the Wolf Man, who began treatment in 1910 and whose case was followed up over sixty years (by Freud and other analysts), and a case of homosexuality in an unnamed young woman – another very short-term treatment. Each of these cases has its own fascinating features and bears much close analysis. In this chapter I will discuss the four cases individually. For the sake of argument, I will divide Freud's case histories into two categories: the extended or 'successful' cases, and the short or prematurely broken off treatments. Coincidentally, these two categories seem to align themselves naturally with his treatment of men and his treatment of women. By looking at Freud's (relative) successes with men and his (relative) failures with women we might be able to further isolate Freud's troubling relation to that central question we saw him asking Marie Bonaparte in the last chapter: what do women want?

FREUD'S ANIMAL MEN: THE RAT MAN AND THE WOLF MAN

THE RAT MAN: 'NOTES UPON A CASE OF OBSESSIONAL NEUROSIS' (1909)

The 'Rat Man' was a twenty-nine-year-old lawyer and soldier, Ernst Lanzer, who came to see Freud in 1907 because of his inability to rid himself of his obsessional and upsetting thoughts. He had a continuing dread that he would cut his own throat with a razor. He also obsessively brooded on the idea that something terrible might happen to people he cared most about. He was particularly focused on the possibility of some catastrophe befalling his father or the woman with whom he was in love. Some time into the analysis Freud was astonished to discover that the Rat Man's father, whom he was so afraid of hurting, was in fact already dead. He had died years before the analysis began.

The immediate cause of the Rat Man's seeking analysis, and the source of Freud's strange nickname for him, was a story the Rat Man had heard from a fellow officer. This man had told him about a Chinese torture technique in which a pot was filled with rats and tied to a victim's buttocks: the rats eventually gnawed their way into the victim's anus. The Rat Man had to struggle through much resistance to tell Freud this story, which had upset him greatly. He could hardly get the words out. After hearing of the rat torture, the Rat Man could not rid himself of the thought that this punishment would happen to a person who was dear to him. And yet Freud saw a different reaction mixed in with the Rat Man's disgust and fear: 'At all the more important moments while he was telling his story his face took on a very strange, composite expression. I could only interpret it as one of *horror at pleasure of his own of which he himself was unaware*' (Freud 1909: 47–8).

What became clear to Freud in the course of treating the Rat Man was that one of the keys to obsessive-compulsive disorders was the presence of violently ambivalent feelings towards those who are consciously loved and admired. That look that suffused the Rat Man's face, of 'horror at pleasure of his own of which he himself was unaware', expressed the turmoil that takes place emotionally between conscious disgust and unconscious desire. The pleasure can be seen as sadistic (a secret desire for this punishment to happen to others), but it also might contain an element of masochism (the story becomes sexually thrilling; the erotic charge of imagining himself penetrated combines with the hideousness of the form of penetration). The consciously inadmissible desire to hurt others collides with a desire to be punished himself for having these unacceptable thoughts.

The Rat Man's intense fears about something terrible happening to his father, even after his death, were similarly related to his hostile feelings towards his father. Like the neurotic, the obsessive-compulsive has wishes and strong emotional reactions that he cannot consciously admit. Instead he turns these wishes around: the thought that the Rat Man might like to inflict pain on someone made him feel guilty, as if he had actually done something to that person rather than just fantasised about it. To protect his threatened love objects against the violence and terror of his own mind, the Rat Man constructed a belief system in which only his carefully controlled thoughts, or his obsessive actions, could keep the threatened person safe.

An authority figure such as a father may die in reality but live on as a frightening or punishing paternal image in the unconscious of his child. Obsessive-compulsives, Freud found, refuse to separate thought from reality. They believe strongly in the power of their own thoughts to kill off others or to keep them alive. Obsessives also fear the magical effects of others' thoughts on themselves. As a child the Rat Man believed that his parents knew his thoughts and fantasies without him telling them, and that punishment would follow from the impurity of these thoughts. For the young Rat Man, someone he loved was bound to be punished for any sexual urges he had. For instance, if he wished to see a woman naked, the wish would be followed by the unshakable feeling that his father might die because of the wish (Freud 1909: 43).

In order to ward off the imagined catastrophic effects of the Chinese rat torture – to keep the torture from happening to his father or his beloved – the Rat Man developed an unbelievably complicated series of rules and actions that he was required to follow. In his case history Freud retells the details of the Rat Man's rituals, which take on a religious and self-punishing quality – his obsessive actions and designs are all to fend off the underlying reality of his own hostile wishes. In reality, when he was alive the Rat Man's father had been judgemental about the woman the Rat Man loved. In line with his theory of the Oedipus complex, Freud found that, even after his father's death, the Rat Man saw his father as a hostile interferer in his love relations. Yet his childhood love, admiration and fear of this image of his father, that he still felt, required him to try and please his father as well.

An example may be the best way to describe how this complicated mix of emotions manifests itself in an obsessive. One of the Rat Man's many routines developed at the time he was studying for his college examinations. He would always make sure that he was awake and working between the hours of midnight and one, when he imagined that his father (who was by then already dead) might put in a ghostly appearance. Between twelve and one the Rat Man would open the front door of his flat for his father, then re-enter his house, take out his penis and stand looking at it in front of the mirror. This bizarre behaviour makes psychic sense according to Freud if we see it as combining two opposing wishes. When the Rat Man's father was alive he had often complained that his son didn't work hard enough. By imagining his father returning at such a late hour, and finding him still up and working, the Rat Man includes a fantasy of pleasing his father in his night-time routine. On the other hand, it is doubtful that his father would have been overjoyed to return home and find his son masturbating. In this aspect of his behaviour the Rat Man defies his father and his father's disapproval of his love life. One obsessional act carries the weight of both love and hate for the parent – reconfirming Freud's idea in the Oedipus complex of the male child's antagonism towards the father, and embodying in each element of the obsessional fantasy a contradictory impulse.

Another example of one of the Rat Man's obsessive activities also displays the potential of psychoanalytic reading. One summer, when the Rat Man was on vacation, he couldn't get out of his mind the obsessive idea that he was too fat and that he had to lose weight. He began running for long distances, climbing harsh mountainsides and skipping dessert in order to lose weight. One session with Freud produced a productive chain of associations for the Rat Man. The German word for fat is *dick*, which was also the name of an American cousin of his. It emerged that his cousin Dick was paying attention to a young woman with whom the Rat Man was also infatuated. When the Rat Man tried to get rid of his fat he was really trying to get rid of his cousin – in his harsh punishing work-out regime he could be seen to be punishing his cousin as well as himself.

Freud viewed the Rat Man as one of his most successful cases. He succeeded in ridding the Rat Man of his tormenting repetitive thoughts by uncovering the root causes in his difficult relation to his childhood sexual urges – his sexual experimentation with a governess and his fear of his father's anger if he found out. Freud's final footnote on the Rat Man case points to the great and tragic distance that lies between inner and outer reality, the distance that the obsessive himself cannot initially recognise. Freud writes, in the final footnote to the case: 'The patient's mental health was restored to him by the analysis which I have reported upon in these pages. Like so many other young men of value and promise, he perished in the Great War' (Freud 1909: 128). World War I prevented the possibility of observing whether the Rat Man maintained his hard-won mental health – history cut short the psychoanalytic cure.

Freud's work with the Rat Man showed that the obsessive's tortured rituals embody doubled desires which are at odds with each other, and also that these rituals rely on difficulty in distinguishing the inner world from the outer world – although the Rat Man's father had died years before he began analysis, he was still a powerful and punishing figure in his child's psychic world. Another of Freud's patients, the Wolf Man, similarly displayed obsessive fears and anxieties, but also a host of other symptoms. If the state of the Rat Man's mental health could never be finally ascertained because of his premature death, the Wolf Man lived, perhaps, too long, in the shadow of his identity as Freud's most famous patient.

THE WOLF MAN: 'FROM A HISTORY OF AN INFANTILE NEUROSIS' (1918)

Another of Freud's surprisingly named patients, the Wolf Man, was in reality a wealthy young Russian named Sergei Pankeiev. Pankeiev was treated by Freud and other analysts for depression and obsessional symptoms throughout his life. He lived until 1979 and reputedly answered the phone with 'Wolf Man here', adopting for himself the identity under which Freud made him strangely famous.

The Wolf Man's name issued from a nightmare he had as a child that resulted in a phobic fear of wolves. In his dream he was terrified by the sight of six or seven white wolves perching on the branch of a walnut tree outside his bedroom window. Freud took this dream as the root cause of the neurosis which plagued his patient throughout early childhood; he and the Wolf Man spent a large amount of analytic time analysing it. In an extremely complicated and (it has to be said) often unconvincing interpretation of the Wolf Man's wolf dream and resulting phobia, Freud maintained that the dream was a distortion of a scene that the Wolf Man had witnessed when he was only a tiny child, perhaps one-and-a-half years old: a scene of his father having sexual intercourse with his mother from behind. This child's eye view of his parents locked in a sexual embrace Freud called the primal scene, and he suggested that it was one possible trigger for the Oedipus complex. However, even within the bounds of the case itself, Freud swayed back and forth on the status of the primal scene – arguing at one moment that the baby must have really witnessed this scene, at the next that the baby might have just fantasised his parents' sexual activity. The question of the visual – what the young child actually sees and what he or she simply imagines – is one that Freud always returns to, often with conflicting answers.

For Freud the Wolf Man's case history firmly supported his ideas about childhood sexuality, and the possibility of developing neurosis (which, as we know, always contains a sexual component) even in earliest childhood. As a very young child the Wolf Man went through a pious, obsessive period which coincided with his excessive fear of wolves and other animals. He remembered his older sister tormenting him with a particular picture of a wolf. Through the techniques of analysis Freud was able to ascertain that at a very early age the Wolf Man's older sister initiated him into sexual practices. Although his sister was in reality much more aggressive than he, in his own fantasies the Wolf Man imagined himself the aggressive one and his sister the passive recipient of his attentions (Freud 1918: 248).

As in the *Rat Man*, Freud found in the Wolf Man's case a continuing vacillation between active and passive desires. Freud imagined that the young child might misinterpret the scene of his parents' intercourse as an attack on the mother by the father, similarly enacting these fluctuating anxieties about activity and passivity, love and violence. These early sexual disturbances were, of course, seen as central to the childhood and adult pathologies that later develop.

One compelling aspect of the case of the Wolf Man is Freud's analytic and rhetorical techniques. He must convince two audiences of the validity of his interpretations: his patient and his readers. At times the methods which Freud uses to interpret the Wolf Man's dream about the wolves seem to rely on a topsy-turvy, almost *Alice in Wonderland*-like, logic. For instance, the Wolf Man says that in his dream the wolves were totally still and staring at him with 'strained attention' (Freud 1918: 263). Through the distortions of dream logic Freud transposes the stillness of the wolves into its opposite – claiming that, instead of immobility, the Wolf Man must have woken to a scene of violent motion, and, instead of being looked at, the baby must himself have stared intently at the scene. From these meagre beginnings Freud constructs the powerful primal scene that he claims the child must have viewed.

The interpretation of the Wolf Man's dream about the wolves involves an understanding of the importance of **construction** to analysis.

CONSTRUCTION

A construction is an interpretation by the analyst which may seem far-fetched and removed from the immediate analytic material. The goal of

> the construction is to bring up repressed childhood material which may
> have been a real experience of the patient, or may have been fanta-
> sised by the patient, but which contains something important to the
> patient's later development: 'scenes [like the Wolf Man's witnessing of
> his parents' sexual intercourse] which date from such an early period …
> and which further lay claim to such an extraordinary significance for the
> history of the case, are as a rule not reproduced as recollections, but
> have to be divined – constructed – gradually and laboriously from an
> aggregate of indications' (Freud 1918: 248).

Many later readers of the case have questioned Freud's interpretation of the Wolf Man's dream, including the Wolf Man himself, who,
in an interview conducted late in his life, denied ever having fully
believed Freud's interpretation. In retrospect it seems that any positive
psychoanalytic influence on the Wolf Man had more to do with the
Wolf Man's transference on to Freud than it did with Freud's correct
reading of his patient's early life and childhood neuroses. Freud acted
as a father figure for the Wolf Man, lending him money and giving
him advice, not the types of activities that are now accepted in analysts, who are expected to remain aloof from intimate relationships
with their patients. It is probable that the interpretations of the Wolf
Man's wolf dream originated entirely with Freud.

The Wolf Man case was never as much of a therapeutic triumph for
Freud as the written record makes it out to be. The Wolf Man continued to have treatment for obsessional neurosis and depression for
the rest of his life, and in fact he seems to have developed a fixation
on his status as Freud's famous patient, immortalised primarily for his
illness. Despite its shortcomings as a cure, the ideas that emerge from
the case of the Wolf Man are crucial to the further development of
analytic theory and practice. The concept of constructions, the often
theoretically productive difficulty in pinning down the status of childhood memories and dream material as fantasy or reality, and the
question of the influence that the analyst's suggestions can have on the
patient, are central psychoanalytic problems that the Wolf Man's case
history brings up. The Wolf Man and the Rat Man were both cases to
which Freud devoted a lot of time and energy; his sympathy, his
paternal care and sometimes his admiration for his patients' creativity
and stamina in confronting their illnesses come through in his

discussions of their debilitating neurotic problems. It is fair to see that Freud, at times, identifies with the creative but tortured illnesses of his male patients. A different attitude emerges in Freud's case histories of women, to which we will now turn.

FREUD'S TROUBLE WITH WOMEN: DORA, AND A CASE OF FEMALE HOMOSEXUALITY

DORA: 'FRAGMENT OF AN ANALYSIS OF A CASE OF HYSTERIA' (1905)

The case of 'Dora' was originally recorded by Freud in 1901 from a patient he saw in 1900. Dora was in reality an eighteen-year-old girl named Ida Bauer, brought by her father to see Freud against her own inclination. She was suffering from recurrent depression, fits of coughing, fainting spells and the periodic loss of her voice, amongst other hysterical symptoms. She had become withdrawn from her father, with whom she had once been close, and she was on very bad terms with her mother. Dora's father brought her to Freud after they found a note in her desk declaring her intention of committing suicide. Freud quickly discovered a complicated sexual and emotional triangle (or square) that included the girl – though it was not of her making – that had obviously affected her deeply.

The situation was as follows. Dora's whole family, but especially her father and herself, were very close to a couple, Herr and Frau K., whom they had met at a health resort that Dora's father had attended to try and cure his tuberculosis. It emerged quite early in the analysis that Dora was aware that Frau K. and her father were having an affair. Yet Frau K. was also intimate friends with Dora, and Dora looked after the K.s' children, becoming 'almost a mother to them'. Dora was also very friendly with Herr K. When she was fourteen Herr K. made sexual advances towards Dora, which she spurned. This did not, however, seem much to affect the general intercourse between the two families. When Herr K. again propositioned Dora two years later she again reacted negatively and with another bout of hysterical symptoms. Her father, at this point, brought her to see Freud.

The setting for Dora's illness – her convoluted family relations – reads like a late Victorian melodrama full of sexual intrigue and unspeakable suspicions. By telling Freud her family history, Dora exposed the adult affairs that surrounded her and protested her unwilling place in the scheme of events. Dora told Freud that she felt that her father and Frau K. had offered her to Herr K. to appease him; if Herr K. agreed to overlook Frau K.'s affair with Dora's father, Dora's father would hand over Dora for Herr K.'s pleasure. It is a sordid and upsetting tale to read now about a girl who was between fourteen and sixteen at the time when most of these events occurred. Freud accepts Dora's version of the events – he explicitly does not believe the version that Dora's father proffers, that Dora simply fantasised Herr K.'s advances. And yet Freud is also part of the chain of powerful adults who treat Dora as an object of exchange. Freud describes how Dora's father 'handed her over to me for psychotherapeutic treatment' (Freud 1905a: 49). With this 'handing over' Freud, too, becomes a player in the drama of Dora, reshaping her story to suit the needs of his psychoanalytic theory.

Unlike Freud's doctor–patient relationship with the Rat Man or the Wolf Man, Dora and Freud had a combative relationship from the beginning. The case history of Dora has been seen as a struggle between Dora and Freud to tell the story of Dora's hysteria. Freud's treatment of Dora is fascinating but often quite upsetting to read about. In my earlier discussion of *Studies on Hysteria* I talked of the ways in which hysterics suffer from gaps in their memories. The traumatic origins of their repressed desires are lost or missing. They themselves often seem like fragmented persons, unable to use their native language, or sometimes even their own limbs. One goal of psychoanalytic therapy was to help fill in these gaps in women hysterics' stories – to make them readable to themselves. Listening to what the patient had to say about her dreams and free associations allowed Freud to suggest new versions of the contents of the patient's mind and the actions of the patient's body. But there is a danger in this sort of activity, as we have seen in the case of the Wolf Man; the story that the analyst wants to tell about the patient may not always be identical to the story the patient tells about him or herself. The analyst, with his claims to being able to unlock the secrets of the unconscious, can seem quite powerful in relation to the patient; his story may appear to be the more convincing one, particularly when it is backed up by an impressive medical diagnosis and an official case history.

Freud's writing up of Dora's case contains many moments when Dora disagrees with his interpretations. The most crucial instance of this is Freud's insistence to Dora that she was actually in love with Herr K., and that her hysteria came in part from her own repressed feelings for him. Dora denies this explanation of Freud's for much of the therapy, but eventually capitulates to his interpretation, and most of the therapy reads like a battle of wills. For instance, he finds her reactions of disgust to Herr K.'s advances on her when she is fourteen years old 'already entirely and completely hysterical' (Freud 1905a: 59). Dora must have been attracted to him, Freud reasons (even stating, admiringly, that Herr K. is a very attractive man), so how could she have spurned his advances? According to Freud, it was because she reacted to him with a hysterical reversal of affect, she repressed her desire for Herr K. and reacted in the opposite way to her unconscious desires.

Freud's interpretations of Dora's dreams are a *tour de force* of detective prowess which I highly recommend reading. Yet Freud's interpretations also seem brutal, forced and insensitive. Dora's repeated complaints that she does not recall feeling the way Freud insists she must have felt bring forth his virulent insistence upon the superior interpretative power of the analyst, who can delve into the depths of the unconscious. If Dora says No, she really means Yes, because 'there is no such thing at all as an unconscious "No"' (Freud 1905a: 92). Any associations that Dora has with anything that Freud suggests can be turned around to prove his point. Any protest, at least in this case history, is filed by Freud under resistance or repression – as an idea that hasn't made it past the unconscious into consciousness yet. It seems that resistance really is futile in psychoanalysis, at least if you are Dora.

Hélène Cixous, the French psychoanalytic literary critic, describes Dora as 'the core example of the protesting force of women' (Bernheimer and Kahane 1985: 1). Dora became an exemplary feminist heroine, in a sense, by walking out on Freud. Her case is a fragment because she refused to complete her analysis. By doing so, she denied Freud the possibility of an unfragmented, complete story. In Freud's earlier case from *Studies on Hysteria*, 'Elizabeth von R.', he claims that 'the whole work was, of course, based on the expectation that it would be possible to establish a completely adequate set of determinants for the events conceived' (Freud and Breuer 1895: 207). This assumption implies that a full set of facts – if the analyst is able to achieve knowledge of them – will yield a complete understanding of the determining factors of a case of hysteria. But, as we have seen in Freud's sometimes contradictory attitude towards dream interpretation, psychoanalytic theorising can also dispute the possibility of ever being able to gain 'a full set of facts'.

Within the bounds of the case history, which is obviously written by Freud, Dora appears to dispute Freud's sense of mastery, his claim to total knowledge of her. She finally tells Freud that she is quitting, opening one of her sessions with the following words:

'Do you know that I am here for the last time today?' – 'How can I know, as you have said nothing to me about it?' – 'Yes, I made up my mind to put up with it till the New Year. But I shall wait no longer than that to be cured.' – 'You know that you are free to stop the treatment at any time. But for today we will go on with our work. When did you come to this decision?' – 'A fortnight ago, I think.' 'That sounds like a maidservant or a governess – a fortnight's notice.'

(Freud 1905a: 146)

Freud finds himself in the position of a dismissed maid or governess, feminised and made as powerless as a servant by Dora's refusal to take part any longer in the analytic scene. Dora's case can be seen as a power struggle amongst an intriguing cast of characters – Freud, Dora, Dora's father, Herr K. and Frau K. – over who will control the narrative and set the terms for the truth of what happened and the true causes of Dora's hysteria.

Dora's deepest fury is at not being believed when she tells her father about Herr K.'s advances:

None of her father's actions seems to have embittered her so much as his readiness to consider the scene by the lake as a product of her imagination. She was almost beside herself at the idea of its being supposed that she had merely fancied something on that occasion.

(Freud 1905a: 79)

The trouble with psychoanalysis as it is used by Freud in *Dora* is that it promises that a therapist will listen to, and work with, the stories of the hysteric, but it then also breaks that promise. On the one hand, Freud recognises that sexual intrigues do happen, that young girls and older men are sometimes involved, and that everyone in late Victorian society except for the shamelessly blunt analyst seems to have a vested interest in keeping these sexual scandals under wraps. Freud treats

Dora's story with a certain amount of respect; he believes that she has been used as a bargaining chip in her father's intrigues, and he sees that understanding the events between her, the K.s and her father will be central to understanding her sickness and curing it. On the other hand, Freud, by claiming expert knowledge of the unconscious, also claims to know what Dora wants better than she does herself, and claims that what she wants is Herr K. – an older man, a substitute for her own father. When Dora quits the treatment and refuses to listen to any more of Freud's stories, she impels him to try and understand what went wrong, what it was that he did not understand about Dora's desires.

The positive discovery that comes out of the failure of Dora's treatment, for Freud, is his fuller recognition of transference. Transferences, if you recall, were the impulses and fantasies that are aroused during the analysis and directed towards the analyst. These impulses and fantasies always, as Freud puts it, 'replace some earlier person by the person of the physician' (Freud 1905a: 157). Freud realises, too late, that he neglected to take into account the kinds of transferences that Dora was making on to him – that she was in fact acting out her hostility towards Herr K. by abandoning her therapy. What Freud is less capable of realising is the kind of transferences (or counter-transferences) that he himself makes on to Dora. Comparing Freud's aggressive reactions to Dora with his supportive discussions of the Rat Man, one can see that there are very different emotions at work in each case.

In a footnote to the case, Freud also recognises another factor that he believes contributed to his failure in the case of Dora. He realises that he overestimated Dora's erotic and emotional attachment to men (her father and Herr K.) and underestimated her erotic attachment to one particular woman, Frau K. It becomes clear that Dora's knowledge of sexual matters has come to her through Frau K., that they were on intimate terms, and that Dora may have felt just as betrayed by her as she did by her own father and Herr K. Freud at the end of the case admits to his own blindness to this fact: 'I failed to discover in time and to inform the patient that her homosexual (gynaecophilic) love for Frau K. was the strongest unconscious current in her mental life' (Freud 1905a: 162). Homosexuality is a problem for Freud. It is not that he refuses to admit its existence, or even that he views it as a patho-logical illness. As we have seen in the last chapter in his *Three Essays on Sexuality*, Freud recognises that the development towards heterosexuality is no more 'natural' or necessary than the development towards homosexuality. But his narrative of sexual development – the Oedipus complex – still leads him to downplay homosexual attachments in favour of the primacy of heterosexual ones. The next case history brings to the forefront the question of homosexuality and how psychoanalysis approaches it.

'THE PSYCHOGENESIS OF A CASE OF HOMOSEXUALITY IN A WOMAN' (1920)

The last case history that Freud published involved an eighteen-year-old homosexual girl who was brought to him after a suicide attempt. Homosexuality at the time was criminalised by law and stigmatised as a disease by both the medical profession and the newly emerging profession of sexology. Although there were some sympathetic commentators who were exceptions to this rule, homosexuality was usually at best treated as an illness which required sympathy, pity and possibly therapy to help convince homosexuals of the error of their ways (see Weeks 1980). Freud's attitudes need to be contextualised in the light of the attitudes that surrounded him, so that we can understand some of the more impressive aspects of his attitude to this young woman.

Like Dora, 'A Case of Female Homosexuality' (as it is popularly known) involved a reluctant analysand. The girl did not feel that she needed psychoanalytic treatment and resisted coming to see Freud. As Freud points out, an unwilling patient greatly lessens the chance of psychoanalytic success. The girl's father forced her to see Freud after she had thrown herself on to a suburban railway line. In the circumstances that immediately preceded the incident, the girl's father had spotted her on the street with a woman with whom she was in love, and clearly registered his anger and disgust. One of Freud's achievements in his treatment of her was to recognise that the girl's attempted suicide was not necessarily related to her homosexuality, except in so far as it was a reaction to feeling rejected by her father. In other words, she was not unhappy because she was homosexual, she was unhappy because being a homosexual at that time could mean ostracisation from one's family.

Freud writes that there were many factors in the case that made it seem unlikely that it would resolve itself in a cure, but the primary one was that he did not think she needed to be cured, at least not of her homosexuality:

> the girl was not in any way ill (she did not suffer from anything in herself, nor did she complain of her condition) and ... the task to be carried out did not consist in resolving a neurotic conflict but in converting one variety of the genital organisation of sexuality into the other.
>
> (Freud 1920a: 375)

Freud recognises that this desire for a 'cure' for her homosexuality, which made her father bring her to him in the first place, is a misplaced desire. The most that psychoanalysis could do, Freud suggests, would be to restore a sense of original childhood bisexuality, but even this is quite unlikely. Since homosexuality, like heterosexuality, involves choosing to give up one love object (either the mother or the father) and keep the other, the two developmental paths are not structurally very different from each other:

> One must remember that normal sexuality too depends upon a restriction in the choice of object. In general, to undertake to convert a fully developed homosexual into a heterosexual does not offer much more prospect of success than the reverse, except that for good practical reasons the latter is never attempted.
>
> (Freud 1920a: 375–6)

'Practical' reasons are not 'natural' reasons. Obviously it was easier to live in the world of early twentieth-century Vienna (as it is still easier to live in the world of early twenty-first century Europe and America) as a heterosexual rather than a homosexual. By foregrounding the contingent development of both these sexual attitudes Freud points out that they are roughly equivalent, and suggests that both of them depend upon ruling out certain object choices. Heterosexuality and homosexuality are not judged by Freud in terms of their pathology or normality; rather they are seen as choices that are made by people consciously and unconsciously. All that psychoanalysis claims to contribute to sexual choice is an analysis of the family dynamics from which these choices emerge.

In the course of the analysis Freud discovers that the girl's early intense love object was her mother; she decided to make herself like a man in order to win her mother's love. According to Freud's analysis, the girl appeared coolly reserved towards her father, but in fact she harboured feelings of revenge and hatred towards him. An exasperated

Freud finds that she displays the same unemotional attitude towards the analysis and his insights that she does towards her father: 'Once when I expounded to her a specially important part of the theory, one touching her very nearly, she replied in an inimitable tone, "How very interesting," as though she were a *grande dame* being taken over a museum and glancing through her lorgnon at objects to which she was completely indifferent' (Freud 1920a: 390). Like Dora, this patient's resistance to his readings of her situation appears to upset Freud – he is taken out of the position of master or all-knowing analyst by the frank indifference of his audience. Freud suggests that the girl has transferred her feelings towards her father on to Freud and is treating him with a similar icy disdain. Because of this disdain, other, more emotionally engaged, kinds of transference will be unable to develop. Therefore, Freud breaks off the treatment after a short time and advises the girl's parents to send her to a woman doctor with whom the girl may be more willing to develop positive transferences.

'A Case of Homosexuality in a Woman' is a brief but interesting case history that displays both Freud's strengths and his shortcomings. Theoretically his attitude towards homosexuality is unpathologising and sympathetic. But his practical attitude towards his women patients, such as Dora and the eighteen-year-old homosexual girl, betrays a difficult wrestling with the problem of femininity: Freud's inability to make his women patients' past memories conform completely to his theories of the Oedipus complex.

SUMMARY

Freud's case histories are some of the best places to look for his most brilliant interpretative turns and his literary finesse. His analyses are powerful and persuasive pieces of rhetoric that are full of psychological insight, although, as we have seen, they can also seem brutal or forced. According to Freud, the Rat Man's obsessive-compulsive disorders were acted out in reaction to a series of ambivalent emotions, particularly towards his dead father; guilt and hatred went hand in hand with admiration and shame. The Wolf Man's infantile dream of the wolves outside his window contributes the idea of the primal scene, and further fuels a continuing argument about the relative importance of memory and reconstruction in analysis. 'Dora' and 'A Case of Female

Homosexuality' both display Freud's practical mishandling of young women patients, at the same time as they show his theoretical flair for interpretation. In the end, Freud may have stopped writing case histories because he was in fact more interested in his theories than in his practice. After 1920 many of Freud's theoretical writings theorise and systematise the shape and working of the psyche. These ideas of Freud's often return to the concept that physical processes can be measured in terms of the circulation and distribution of instinctual energies – the increase and decrease of instinctual drives. It is to Freud's ideas about mapping the workings of the mind, often called his economic theories, that I now turn.

5

FREUD'S MAPS OF THE MIND

As a theoriser Freud was attracted to dualistic explanations: he divided problems into two opposing forces or two antagonistic terms. Conflict is at the centre of psychoanalytic thinking – the battle between conflicting conscious and unconscious desires causes the repression which leads to neurosis. Children both love and hate their parents – violent and erotic feelings often accompany each other in infancy. If these emotions are not satisfactorily resolved, the contending forces set the grounds for the adult's psychic difficulties, as we have seen in Freud's case histories. The simultaneous existence of opposing emotions and urges is a consistent theme of psychoanalytic theory (see the definition of ambivalence, p. 53).

During the latter 1910s and the early 1920s Freud extensively revised and rethought psychoanalytic theory. He changed his ideas about what constituted the primary instinctual urges of humanity. Although his desire for dualistic explanations led him to attempt to simplify the number of terms he worked with, he often found himself adding yet another term to his dualistic concepts instead. In this chapter I will cover the question of these shifting psychoanalytic maps of the mind, and the terminology which Freud used in his attempt to create a totalising explanation of human psychic life. I will focus on two main interrelated Freudian templates: that of the instincts, and that of the structure of the mental apparatus which Freud divided into those well known but often misunderstood terms ego, id and super-ego. The word 'instinct' is the English translation of the German word *Trieb* that is used in the Standard Edition of Freud's works. However the word 'drive' is used more frequently nowadays to translate *Trieb*, in order to distinguish Freud's idea of instincts from the instincts of animals. Throughout this chapter I use 'drive' and 'instinct' interchangeably.

Before I begin my exploration of these two schemas, however, I want to call attention to one interesting paradox about Freud's desire to map the mind. In attempting to systematise and categorise sexuality and its accompanying energies, Freud often appears to install a set of universal rules – a scientific explanation for the workings of human sexuality. However, to do so, he and other nineteenth-century sexologists consistently borrow names from literature – there is the Oedipus complex, named after *Oedipus the King*; narcissism, named after the mythical figure Narcissus; masochism, named after the punishment-loving Sacher-Masoch, author of the erotic novel *Venus in Furs*; and sadism, named after the French philosopher of the bedroom, the Marquis de Sade. Literary stories seem like unlikely places to look to extract a scientific explanation or system. Literature is stereotypically seen as the opposite of science – more interested in fantasy than truth, and untrammelled by a need for accuracy. The fact that Freud often finds the inspiration for his theories of sex and the mind in the realm of literature should alert us to the ways in which the two studies can reciprocally affect each other, even when we approach the more 'scientific' Freud (Felman 1977a: 9).

NARCISSISM, EGO AND ID

Narcissism was a term originally used by Freud to describe the sexual attitude in which a person directs his love towards himself, rather than towards another. Narcissus was a Greek mythological figure who fell in love with his own reflection in a pool of water and became rooted to the spot, staring at his own image, until he eventually found himself turned into a flower for his trouble. Narcissism, like many of Freud's terms that began their lives referring to perversions or pathologies, eventually extended its meaning as Freud recognised that love of oneself and erotic interest in one's own body were in fact a normal and healthy stage of individual development. By no means all self-love can be considered pathological: indeed, a degree of self-love is necessary for everyone. The phase of infantile narcissism, in which the child takes himself as a sexual object and bestows his love on himself, is an extension of the even earlier period when the child could not distinguish between himself and the outside world, when he could not tell where the breast ended and he began. As the child grows up he discovers the sexual correlate of this infantile self-love – the auto-erotic satisfaction of masturbation.

When Freud begins thinking about the importance of narcissism he complicates a model he has developed of the **instincts**.

INSTINCTS

Instincts are energetic bodily drives to certain kinds of action. All instincts originally have biological sources – the aim of every instinct is satisfaction, which it attempts to find in objects – the people, things, body parts, etc., one looks towards to satisfy erotic desires.

Until he postulates the existence of narcissism Freud has assumed that there are two separate sets of instincts which guide all human activities: instincts of self-preservation (connected with the **ego**) and sexual instincts (connected with the libido or **id**). His ideas about the ego and the id change over the course of his many explorations of the topic, and they change in relation to each other (see Freud 1923). It is also important to remember that Freud never actually used 'id', 'ego' or 'super-ego' himself. It was his primary English translator, James Strachey, who took Freud's German terms, *das Es* (the It), *das Ich* (the I) and *das Über Ich* (the Over-I) and translated them as 'id', 'ego' and 'super-ego'. One effect of Strachey's Latinate translations was to make Freud's commonplace language seem more scientific. For clarity's sake, I will stick to a few basic definitions.

The ego, id and super-ego are topographical concepts – meaning that they exist 'within' the mind, but that their existence could never be marked out on specific parts of the brain. (For a definition of the super-ego see p. 45.) Topography refers to mapping. Freud's maps of the mind are, in a sense, imaginary: they cannot be traced out on the material of the body or the brain. Rather, Freud's topographies per-form the service of helping us understand the way these areas of the psyche work together and relate to each other.

EGO AND ID

When the child is first born it is a mass of id, an amorphous, unstructured set of desires; the demand 'I want' is the sum total of its mind's contents. Out of these primal desires an ego quickly begins to emerge. One definition of ego is the individual's image of himself as a self-conscious being, his sense of himself as separate from the world which surrounds him. Another psychoanalytic definition of ego is that which is conscious in the person, that which experiences and senses the outside world and which represents reality to the self. These two meanings are related but not identical – the first meaning of ego is more encompassing: it implies a whole self, rather than a self which is split into separate, warring factions, the ego and the id, that the other meaning implies.

The id is inseparable from the unconscious – id wants and desires in the here-and-now, it doesn't make plans for the future. Freud often claims that the unconscious (which is the same as the id) knows no time but the present, no answer but Yes. The ego, on the other hand, recognises time and the setbacks which go along with living in a world where one has to wait. The ego preserves the self by telling it to hold back on its desires and negotiate with reality. The id and the ego roughly line up with two separate sets of instincts – the id correlates to the instinct for pleasure – which Freud also calls Eros, the Greek word for love. (We will have more to say about pleasure in the next section of this chapter, on the pleasure principle.) The ego correlates to the instinct to protect oneself, the instinct of self-preservation.

Freud initially posits these two instincts as separate from each other and as fulfilling two different functions in the psyche. The id says 'I want', and the ego tells it to wait; the id says 'Go for it', and the ego says 'Protect and preserve yourself – survival is more important than instant gratification.' Narcissism, however, appears to bring together these two sets of instincts – if you have enough self-love you will certainly do a good job at preserving yourself. You will be your own primary object of concern as well as of erotic investment – your main motivating force will be to keep your love object alive, which is, of course, you. This picture makes it clear how the two apparently warring impulses of sexuality and self-preservation can actually meet and merge.

In the usual course of events, Freud believed, narcissism was a phase of development: eventually a person would transfer his love for himself to another object. (As the Oedipus complex indicates, this love would usually come to rest on one of the parents.) However, if a person never transfers his self-love to another, original healthy narcissism can lead to severe psychic distress along the lines of psychosis. A delusional sense of one's own importance, schizophrenia, hallucinations and a paranoid feeling of always being watched are all symptoms of narcissistic psychotic disorders. In the severest narcissistic states the patient finds it impossible to engage with other human beings at all; he has no sense that anyone can exist outside his own mind.

Now, if we think back to the importance of transference as a key element of the psychoanalytic cure, we find that the self-absorption of narcissism disturbs the way it works. Transference depends upon a patient's ability to interact with, and have emotional reactions to, others. If you've never hated or loved your father or mother, you won't be able to put your analyst in your parents' place and work out your reactions to them. A complete victim of a narcissistic psychosis could not develop any relationship to the analyst at all, thus making analysis impossible. Successful analysis requires that one should always react emotionally to the analyst as well as to one's own past. The severest version of narcissism locks a person into a private world. If the one who loves and the love object are one and the same person, there is no other, nor even an image of another – no one to bounce love or hate off.

In practical terms, Freud found that those suffering from severe forms of narcissistic illness were difficult if not impossible to treat, because they could not engage in transference. Furthermore, Freud's theories about narcissism also created a problem for his belief in the separation of the ego and the id. The ego was supposedly split off from sexuality – it covered the domain of non-sexual motivations. But the theory of narcissism destroyed this separation by making the sexual object and the I (the ego) who thought and acted one and the same. The force which worked to preserve the self and the force which created desire became indistinguishable from one another. The consequence of this train of thought of Freud's was that all motivations might be considered sexual.

Freud's critics, both in his own time and recently, have often accused him of being a pan-sexualist – meaning that he believed that all human motivations were finally sexual in nature. To try and counter this mistaken assumption, I argued earlier in the book that Freud's theories are as much about interpretation as they are about sex. We products of the twentieth (and twenty-first) century have often adopted this pan-sexual Freud as the one we know best, and feel most comfortable ridiculing – the sex-obsessed old man who finds phallic symbols everywhere he looks. But there was a time when Freud himself was worried that his conclusions were tending in that direction. At the time that he was working on his instinctual theories he realised that narcissism created a quandary. The theoretical consequences of narcissism made it clear that it was impossible to completely separate the sexual instincts from the ego instincts. Was it that every human motivation was sexual after all?

Freud found a way out of this impasse by renegotiating his categories of the psyche. He suggested that there might be a violent, aggressive and self-destructive element to human nature which could not be explained in the terms he had been using. In the next section of this chapter we will look at another way in which Freud thought about his categories of the ego and the id, through the pleasure principle and the reality principle. Into this new dualism another third term must fall – that is Freud's strange and haunting creation, the death drive.

PLEASURE, REALITY, DEATH

Psychoanalysis is rarely a theory of compromise – you find love and hate together, but they never combine to indifference. Hot and cold stay hot and cold together; they do not make lukewarm water. Yet Freud also knows that, although the psyche is never particularly happy about it, there are moments when compromises must be effected in order for us to survive in the world. Freud's early theory of the instincts illustrates one of these compromises.

Freud's instinctual theory initially suggested that there are two sets of instincts – an instinct towards pleasure and an instinct towards self-preservation – which work together despite their opposite aims. Using an economic model of tension and release to describe pleasure, he thinks of pleasure in terms of the most basic kinds of living organisms – ones made up of one or a few cells – with the most basic kind of feelings (if you can even call them feelings at that level of existence). He postulates that an organism, at its simplest, consists of an inside and an outside – the inside of the organism functions to keep it together as an organism by mastering the stimuli which affect it from the outside. A build-up of tension, in the form of stimuli from the outside, which is unmasterable by the inside is unpleasurable. In this particular model it is in the release of tension that pleasure lies.

The human nervous system is one model that puts this dynamic in place. Freud postulates in his article 'Instincts and their Vicissitudes' (1915) that 'the nervous system is an apparatus which has the function of getting rid of the stimuli that reach it, or of reducing them to the lowest possible level' (Freud 1915b: 116). Freud calls this instinctive desire not to be ruffled or bothered the principle of constancy. He also discusses this principle in relation to dreams in *The Interpretation of Dreams*, chapter 7, sections C and E. One of the functions of the dream, and the dream's hallucinatory fulfilling of wishes, is to keep the dreamer happily dreaming and ergo asleep. This particular aspect of Freud's theory can be understood to mean that what we all want most is to keep on sleeping, something which any student could have told him.

Later Freud admits that not all forms of tension are unpleasurable. The build-up towards sexual release may be seen as a form of plea-surable tension. Yet, as Freud imagines sexuality, the release of tension always needs to happen for the pleasure to really take place. The awkwardness of this model for measuring happiness and unhappiness lies in the fact that Freud is taking a quantitative or economic idea (tension/release) and mapping it on to a qualitative world – humans feel all sorts of complicated and mixed emotions, as psychoanalytic theory is quick to point out. Yet, although it may look initially unconvincing, following Freud through his economic theories of the tension and release of the pleasure principle leads down some inter-esting paths and towards some provocative conclusions.

The pleasure principle is aligned with the libido – the drive towards happiness, wish-fulfilment, the release of sexual energy. What is it, then, that counters pleasure for Freud in the human condition? Why are we not all only seeking pleasure all the time? There are a number of different ways of answering this question. First, not all pleasures or wishes can be satisfied as soon as they are conceived. The infant, if you remember, begins by believing that it lives in a world where its wishes are instantly gratified – where there is no distinction between what goes on its own mind and what the world offers it. But this illusion is quickly shattered. In point of fact the mother with the breast is not always there to feed it and put it into a state of infantile bliss. The world does not always satisfy its desires. This state of frustration of expectation, this confrontation with the outer circumstances which have the power to ruin our imagined joy, Freud calls the reality principle. The infant eventually comes to realise that it must negotiate with this outside world in order for its wishes to be granted. It may be possible to achieve pleasure, but the best way of guaranteeing this may not be to insist that pleasure happens immediately; the baby may have to delay pleasure in order eventually to experience it. We are willing to give up the promise of instant gratification if we think our wishes may come true if we wait. These kinds of deals are made in different ways by everybody every day. If we delay our pleasure and go to work, we get paid, and we can count on having more pleasure (or at least more money with which to purchase pleasure) at the weekend. In Chapter 6 we will see that Freud uses this model of the duelling pleasure and reality principles to explain the repressive contract which forms our sense of civilised society.

In 1920 Freud confronts another set of problems around the economic theories he has been postulating. Up to this point Freud has assumed that everyone's ultimate goal is pleasure; if you get diverted from pleasure in the short run by the reality principle, it is really because pleasure is simply being deferred. Even if consciousness admits the possibility of unpleasure, the unconscious is always instinctively turned towards pleasure in every form. Yet as far back as *The Interpretation of Dreams*, however, Freud found himself confronted with some dreams which seemed particularly unpleasurable, which did not seem to be fulfilling wishes. Often these dreams were repeated – nightmares which happened over and over again. One particularly timely example was that of soldiers suffering from shell-shock from the First World War who repeatedly dreamt about being blown up. The traumatic dreams of shell-shocked patients seemed to put Freud's theory of the pleasure principle in jeopardy. Where is the pleasure in returning unconsciously to a terrible and upsetting situation? Why do we repeat that which we could not stand to experience originally?

Repetition becomes a new and disturbing element in Freud's theories in the 1920s, although there is also a sense in which repetition was always a factor in both the neurosis and the psychoanalytic cure. If neurotic illnesses are rooted in events, memories and fantasies of childhood which were never properly understood at the time, the reason why people cannot leave these memories behind is that they are still living through and with them. Neurotics repeat and replay their pasts – they can't escape from them. Even when they translate them into the bodily symptom of hysteria it is still in the form of a repetition, although it is a repetition that they unconsciously hide from themselves by disguising it.

There is another sense also in which the psychoanalytic cure owes a debt to repetition as a process. The cure involves returning psychically to an upsetting situation, back to the scene of a crime, as it were. The analyst leads the patient back through their memories towards the initial upsetting moment, scene or fantasy, but not so that the patient can blindly repeat the experience of the initial trauma, feeling the same unmasterable emotions. Rather, the analyst helps the patient to repeat the experience in order to understand it. Instead of blind repetition, we have repetition with a difference: the ability to analyse and see the source of the difficulty. Freud calls this process working through, in contrast to simple repetition. (See the discussion of 'Remembering, Repeating and Working Through' in the final chapter, p. 121.)

So we see that repetition is a strategy that can work both for and against psychic health. In *Beyond the Pleasure Principle* Freud muses on the contradictory uses of repetition. He finds himself watching a one-and-a-half-year-old child (in reality his grandson, Ernst) playing a game which Freud calls 'fort/da' (or 'gone/there'). The child repeatedly throws away a spool of string and then brings it back to himself, yelling his baby version of 'fort' and 'da' as he does so ('fort' becomes 'o-o-o-o'). Freud interprets this game as the child's re-enacting in play the painful event of his mother's periodic leaving. When the baby triumphantly brings her back ('da!') or flings her away ('fort!') he can pretend he is in control of his mother's movements, instead of her making decisions without reference to him. The 'fort/da' game, like the psychoanalytic cure itself, involves playing at repetition in order to master a painful situation.

Freud postulates, therefore, that there may be uses for repetition, in that it can help us cope with new, unpleasant or apparently unmasterable data. Repetition turns each new situation into an old one, which we may have already experienced and so know how to handle. But Freud was not completely satisfied with his own explanations. He also postulates a compulsion to repeat which has no such obvious psychic use. He noticed that his grandson seemed to throw the spool away more often than he brought it back, although, as Freud points out, bringing it back, staging the mother's return, would involve more of the compensation of pleasure. Freud felt similarly frustrated by the repetitive dreams of shell-shocked soldiers, which seemed to replay their near-death experiences without actually helping them to master the situation – without making them in any sense healthier because of those dreams. He felt that something was missing from his ideas. Was it possible that repetition could be a psychic end in itself? Something that went against what human beings want, either consciously or unconsciously?

In a controversial formulation, Freud came up with what he called the **death drive** to try and explain these diversions from the pleasure principle which were not meant to delay pleasure to conform to the needs of reality.

THE DEATH DRIVE

Contrary to what its name implies, the death drive is not solely connected with aggressive impulses towards others. Freud initially conceives of it as a drive to destroy the self, rather than a drive to destroy others (although the death drive can lead to violent impulses towards others when an individual turns his or her self-directed unconscious aggression outwards.) But, in Freud's economic theory of the instincts, the death drive is not simply imagined as violent. Rather it strives towards the reduction of tensions to absolute zero. The final goal of the death drive is to reduce life to an inorganic state, a state of absolute stasis. Freud's complicated logic suggests that there may be something perversely desirable about this even if the death drive seems to have no economic explanation in Freud's own terms. There is apparently no payback of pleasure involved in the death drive.

Freudian analysts have often ignored the death instinct – or Thanatos, as it also known, in contrast to Eros (the pleasure principle). But *Beyond the Pleasure Principle*, where the death drive is explained, has been picked up by literary theorists as a compelling text, chiefly for the ways in which Freud connects the idea of repetition with death. In *Beyond the Pleasure Principle*'s metaphysical formulations, death and pleasure do finally come to be associated. Death is the ultimate release of tension; it promises the ultimate experience of stasis and complete calm.

Re-enacting unpleasurable experiences comes to seem like a rehearsal for our own death.

But although our own death may be a goal of the self-destructive urge, in reality the deaths we experience are never our own – they are the deaths of family members, friends, loved ones which we must negotiate. In psychoanalytic practice, the death drive is not usually seen as a very useful economic concept of Freud's. Rather, another theory of death and loss seems more relevant to how we actually experience the death of others. One of Freud's most interesting economic concepts centres around the ways in which it becomes possible, or remains impossible, to 'work through' the death of people we love.

FILLING UP, EMPTYING OUT: 'MOURNING AND MELANCHOLIA' (1917)

Psychoanalytic theory can be seen as made up of successive stories of loss. In Sophocles' play, Oedipus Rex loses his sense of mastery, his kingdom, even his eyes, when he discovers he's been acting out a fate over which he had no control. Freud interprets the play as a rehearsal of another originary loss – the moment when the boy child recognises that he has lost the mother as a love object and must give up on his love for her to submit to the threatening figure of the father. The punishing father, via the castration complex, threatens him with another loss – that of his penis. The little girl, discovering sexual difference, according to Freud, goes through a different series of formative events, but they also involve loss and disappointment – she discovers that she is missing something that boys have, and that her mother is missing it too. According to Freud, she turns away from loving her mother in disgust, because her mother cannot give her a penis, and she turns towards the father because she hopes the father can give her, if not a penis, then a penis substitute – a baby. In the stories that psychoanalysis tells about sexual development, young children are always reacting to loss, real or imaginary: the loss of the illusion that your needs and wishes will be fulfilled as soon as you have them, the loss of the comforting maternal sense of security symbolised by the breast, the loss of the penis via the threat of castration, or the sense for the little girl that that loss has already taken place.

So psychoanalysis suggests that we are constantly reacting to different kinds of real and imagined loss, but how do these losses relate to the loss of a real person that happens with death? In his article 'Mourning and Melancholia' Freud analyses the ways in which people react to the death of a loved one, or the loss of a cherished idea: 'mourning is regularly the reaction to the loss of a loved person, or to the loss of some abstraction which has taken the place of one, such as one's country, liberty, an ideal, and so on' (Freud 1917: 251–2). A normal state of mourning may involve a period of serious distress and depression, but should heal itself in time. Melancholia is the pathological version of mourning. Symptoms of melancholia include 'a profoundly painful dejection, cessation of interest in the outside world, loss of the capacity to love, inhibition of all activity, and a lowering of the self-regarding feelings to a degree that finds utterance in self-reproaches and self-revilings, and culminates in a delusional expectation of punishment' (Freud 1917: 252). As Freud points out, the melancholic resembles the normal mourner in everything but their self-hatred.

Mourning may be a painful process that may include psychic denials of the loss of the loved object – dreams or fantasies in which they still live. But, Freud claims, 'Normally, respect for reality gains the day' (Freud 1917: 253). Over time the reality of the object's loss is accepted, and the object's place in the psychic make-up of the mourner is diminished. The normal mourner eventually begins to lose the feeling that they are carrying around the weight of a great loss. Their own ego can emerge: 'when the work of mourning is completed the ego becomes free and uninhibited again' (Freud 1917: 253).

Melancholia, however, invokes another psychic process, and one more difficult to negotiate. What Freud found was that melancholics harboured unconscious ambivalent feelings towards the lost object. The death of a simultaneously loved and hated parent, or being thrown over by a cruel but admired lover, can result in a severe state of melancholia. Melancholics manifest this loss by displaying self-hatred. Freud makes an important distinction: 'In mourning it is the world which has become poor and empty; in melancholia it is the ego itself' (Freud 1917: 254). The loss is taken on to the self – it is as if a part of the self has died along with the person to whom that part of the self was attached. But why does this happen? Freud claims that the self-reproaches of melancholics are really disguised reproaches directed towards the loved person or object. This loathing of the self is a way for melancholics to unconsciously protect themselves from the feelings of guilt that would surely follow if they were consciously to admit their ambivalence towards the lost object. Instead of expressing these difficult feelings, melancholics identify with the lost object, and may even appear to become that other person by taking on their traits. For instance, a daughter who feels guilt at the death of a mother she secretly disliked could begin to take on characteristics of her mother, or do the things she used to do. Melancholics feel responsible for the death of the object; they feel they have psychically murdered the other person. Taking on the other's traits is a way of repairing this loss in fantasy by bringing the other back to life.

In other words, melancholics cannot admit the reality of the ambivalently loved and hated object's death because they are afraid that they were responsible for the murder. Freud imagines this process of melancholic resurrecting of the object in cannibalistic terms. The extreme identification which follows the loss is called introjection; the ego metaphorically devours the lost object, becoming it by taking it into itself. The cure for melancholia involves the conscious recognition and acceptance of the hostile feelings towards the object. When the melancholic finally admits these feelings he can stop hating himself, and loosen the stranglehold that the dead other seems to hold over him. The economic theory of 'Mourning and Melancholia' suggests a world where people are literally filled up or taken over by the past. The melancholic introjects the psyche of the other and unconsciously attempts to live out his life as that other person in order to make up for the damage that he imagines having done to the object. As a theory, melancholia resembles a ghost story, in which the ghost of the dead past actually invades the self. In Freud's theories loss may be rampant, but those who are lost often return to haunt their survivors.

SUPER-EGO

The melancholic's feverish self-hatred springs from the feeling that we commonly label guilt. Guilt is another crucial element in Freud's theories; it is the key to the term which follows the ego and the id, the super-ego (see initial definition, p. 45). The super-ego is the self-critical aspect of the ego: that which judges the conscious and unconscious decisions of the id and the ego. It develops from the ego in its continued attempts to negotiate with reality. The super-ego measures the real ego of a person against an ego ideal – an ideal image of the self that is based on the earliest narcissistic self-love, before a recognition of any flaws in the self. The super-ego is allied with the sense of conscience; it holds the self up to high moral and social standards which the libido wishes to deny. For the super-ego, the individual lives as part of a community, responding and responsible to others. For the id, the individual lives only for himself and what he or she can get. But all three of Freud's structural concepts, the ego, id and super-ego, function in response to each other.

Paranoid patients who think they are constantly being watched, or believe that someone is reading their thoughts, may suffer from delusions. Yet, Freud claims, these delusions also reflect the real state of psychic affairs: 'This complaint is justified; it describes the truth. A power of this kind, watching, discovering and criticising all our intentions, does really exist. Indeed, it exists in every one of us in normal life' (Freud 1914b: 90). The sense of guilt and fear that emerges from the super-ego's surveillance of the subject originates, like so much in Freud, with the relationship to the parents: 'Originally this sense of guilt was a fear of punishment by the parents, or, more correctly, the fear of losing their love; later the parents are replaced by an indefinite number of fellow-men' (Freud 1914b: 97). The super-ego leads the way from individual psychology to group psychology, emphasising the individual's need to insert him or herself into the demands of a community. And that community is usually first represented by the judging and punishing eyes of the parents.

SUMMARY

As we have seen, Freud postulates more than one topography of the mind. Sometimes he arranges the psyche according to the relations between the ego, libido and super-ego. Sometimes he employs the concepts of the pleasure principle, the reality principle and the death drive. But the wars that rage in each individual's inner psychic apparatus (and the compromises which are made there) inevitably involve a struggle between the urge to immediately fulfil desires and the recognition that this is not always possible. Freud's terminology should always be used with caution, recognising that each of his several mappings of the mind is primarily metaphorical – done in the service of attempting to visualise distinctions which are not located in different areas of the body. These distinctions hold up and break down according to the relations between agencies, as we saw in the way in which the concept of narcissism collapses the pleasure principle and the self-preservative instincts. The super-ego is another one of Freud's third terms which serves to complicate the relationship between the ego and the id. In the next section, on Freud and the social, we will see how Freud's super-ego negotiates with the larger outside world while it continues to represent the harsh voice of conscience as springing from the intro-jected voice of the parents. When psychoanalysis moves from theoris-ing about the individual to theorising about the social it never leaves the family far behind.

6

SOCIETY AND RELIGION

Freud was never one to restrict his writings to the realm of individual psychology. Just as he used his initial analyses of hysterical and neurotic illnesses to formulate a universal theory of sexual and mental development, so he applied his ideas which began as theories of the individual, such as the Oedipus complex and repression, to society at large. Through Freud's numerous articles on anthropology, religion, art and society, psychoanalysis developed into a set of principles that claimed the power to explain aspects of all these fields. Psychoanalysis, in a sense, colonised other areas of theoretical speculation about humans and their relations, although it did so with varying degrees of success. There are no anthropologists today who would see in Freud's anthropological writings anything but evidence of past dubious beliefs about anthropology, but the explanatory stories he posits continue to have power as literary creations or myths for our culture. His writings on war and group psychology pose intriguing speculative answers to questions about the herd instinct in human beings, the origin of outbreaks of organised violence, and the distinctively human ability to identify oneself with an immaterial ideal such as a nation or a cause to the extent of being willing to fight and die for it (see particularly 'Thoughts for the Time on War and Death' and 'Group Psychology and the Analysis of the Ego'). All these problems of human social organisation and bonds seemed to Freud to call out for psychoanalytic explanations.

But, even as Freud claimed the right to add psychoanalytic insight to these far-flung areas of human behaviour, he recognised that psychoanalytic thinking could not claim to explain everything. In fact it would be against one of the major principles of psychoanalysis to do so: 'There are no grounds for fearing that psychoanalysis, which first discovered that psychical acts and structures are invariably overdetermined, will be tempted to trace the origin of anything so complicated as religion to a single source' (Freud 1912–13: 159). The overdetermined nature of dreams and symptoms made it clear that the search for a single source or a single interpretation was a misguided one. Similarly, no single source could explain the complicated complex of ideas which make up the human tendency towards religious belief. On the other hand, there may be good grounds for fearing that Freud will try to trace back phenomena to a single root; supplying that sort of determining origin story is a major temptation for him, and one to which he often succumbs. Freud's psychoanalytic stories constantly posit possible explanations for the beginnings of things – whether it is the origin of neurotic illness or of artistic creativity. One of the first promises of psychoanalysis to its hysterical women patients was that uncovering and understanding the origins of their illnesses in repressed memory would help lead them towards a cure. Even when the strength of this claim was modified in the course of analytic practice, the desire for key-like explanations still maintains a strong hold over Freud's imagination. The more speculative his writings become, the more tempted he seems to be by the possibility of discovering the origins of mental states and social practices. In his desire to master original explanations he resembles the young child who is searching for the answer to the question 'Where do babies come from?' or 'Where do I come from?' Freud often asks, 'When and why did this mental development (neurotic symptom, sense of guilt, feeling of hatred for the father, etc.) happen for the first time?' The roots that he imagines sometimes stretch back further than the life of the single individual towards prehistoric speculations.

Freud shares a faith in a popular nineteenth-century analogy that emerged in part from a misreading of evolutionary theory – the idea that 'ontogeny recapitulates phylogeny' or that the childhood of the individual person resembles the earliest prehistoric stages of humanity. This 'childhood of the race' is believed to have survived in the practices of tribal societies or, as the racially inflected terminology of nineteenth-century anthropology labelled them, 'primitive' peoples.

When it employs metaphors of 'the primitive' and savagery, psychoanalysis can be seen as implicated in the racist language and ideas of the time. But, following Freud, critics of racism have also used psychoanalytical ideas and terminology to help explain the psychic mechanisms of twentieth-century racism. For instance, the French psychiatrist and revolutionary writer Frantz Fanon (1925–61) used psychoanalytic theory to help explain the colonial subject's divided experience of being a black subject under white rule. Fanon's psychoanalytically informed analysis of racism points to the way adopting the coloniser's language shapes and creates the consciousness of the colonised. If a culture identifies blackness as inferior or evil, and a black colonial subject grows up speaking the language of that culture, then he or she will unconsciously share these assumptions. Cultural values are internalised, creating a split and alienated subject: the black man or woman who identifies with the dominant colonising culture, who sees him or herself as a subject, and the black man or woman who is repudiated by that culture, the object of that culture's disgust. Fanon takes Freud's question about the mystery of femininity, 'What does Woman want?' (see p. 55) and rephrases it as 'What does the black man want?' (Fanon 1986: 10). Both questions suggest that they could not be fully answered simply by asking a black man or a woman (although that probably wouldn't be a bad place to start). Both questions suggest that unconscious dynamics of desire and disavowal in relation to ourselves and to others play a large part in creating our images of ourselves. We construct what we are, in part, by identifying and rejecting what we are not, and it is in the fear and mistrust of what we are not that racism emerges. If we follow Freud's logic through it is not simply women, or black men, who are mysterious to themselves and others, but everyone. We produce and secure our identities by identifying with some people and disidentifying with others, and this process is never fully conscious. We will never be able to comprehend the deep roots of racism if we look only to conscious beliefs and effects. As Stuart Hall puts it, 'an account of racism which has no purchase on the inner landscape and the unconscious mechanisms of its effects is, at best, only half the story' (Hall 1996: 17). Freud's ideas about resistance, fantasy, unconscious desire and identification may help us comprehend the strange formations that racism takes in both the oppressors and in the oppressed, who inevitably internalise the racist images that surround them.

So, many of Freud's ideas have been taken up by twentieth-century critics writing about racism and postcolonialism, even while some of Freud's parallels, such as the one between children and savages, are implicated in the racialised discourses of the day. As well as the comparison with children, Freud also saw an important parallel in the practices of 'primitive' peoples and the practices of obsessive-compulsives and neurotics. He looked around the world of late nineteenth/early twentieth-century diseases of the mind and saw distorted reflections, on the one hand, of tribal religious practices and, on the other, of childhood beliefs. For Freud, civilisation always carried with it the vestiges of what it had supposedly left behind – instinctual urges, belief in magic and an overwhelming awe of powerful, godlike figures.

CRIMES AGAINST THE FATHER: *TOTEM AND TABOO* (1912–13)

The subtitle of Freud's article *Totem and Taboo*, 'Some Points of Agreement between the Mental Life of Savages and Neurotics', clearly sets out the terrain it covers. In this lengthy article Freud looks at the ways in which ancient religious practices such as totemism resemble the obsessive, ritualistic actions and thought of modern neurotics. Through this connection Freud comes to formulate an extraordinary founding myth of society. He begins by analysing a number of practices of 'primitive' tribes. At the time, anthropology was a speculative field, encompassing many theories unsupported by fieldwork. Freud's efforts rely on dodgy evidence and come up with historically indefensible, but psychologically intriguing, conclusions. By far the best way to view an article such as *Totem and Taboo* is as a work of literature or creative mythology, although this is not how Freud himself would have seen it. Freud believed that he was uncovering the psychological basis for the origins of important social institutions such as religion and civilisation. *Totem and Taboo* attempts to explain the origin of social bonds between people, the origin of the taboo we place on the dead, and the origin of the sense of guilt or conscience that he will later describe as governed by the super-ego.

The book is split up into four essays. In the first, 'The Horror of Incest', Freud provides an overview of anthropological writing on incest. It is easy to see why anthropological work on incest might intrigue Freud, since early-childhood incestuous desire for the parents is such a crucial element of his theories of sexuality. Surveying work that was done on the rituals and practices of 'primitive' people (such as James Frazer's famous work of nineteenth-century anthropology *The Golden Bough*), Freud finds that the taboo against incest is stronger within tribal life than it is in civilised society. The tribal social system of exogamy requires men and women in a tribe to find sexual partners from outside the tribe or face ostracisation. Sexual partners from within the tribe are prohibited or considered taboo. Exogamy is connected with the practice of a tribe, or part of a tribe, of adopting a common totem animal for religious purposes. A totem is a specific animal that is sacred to a tribe because it is believed to carry the tribe spirit. A member of one totem is forbidden to mate with a fellow member of the totem – the exogamous rules of the totem require that they look outside their own group. The totem animal is never hunted, and it is considered very bad luck if one is killed mistakenly. Yet usually, on one sacred occasion during the year, the tribe will ritually slaughter and eat its totem animal. Each member of the tribe symbolically takes into his or her self the admired traits of the totem. As we saw in 'Mourning and Melancholia', an imagined cannibalistic ingestion of a spirit of a person or thing exists as one of the mind's strategies for dealing with loss. Freud finds the similarities between certain psychic developments and these tribal rituals intriguing.

Freud sees the totem object as being subject to a strong sense of ambivalence; once again, we see that negotiating ambivalent feelings is central to psychoanalytic theorising. Something which is forbidden to be touched throughout the year becomes that which is sacrificed and eaten on one sacred occasion; that which is loved and feared becomes that which is destroyed. The second part of *Totem and Taboo*, 'Taboo and Emotional Ambivalence', looks at the ways in which the structure of these primitive religious rites are mirrored by the beliefs of obsessive-compulsives. Taboo, originally a Polynesian word, means that something is sacred and consecrated, but therefore forbidden and unapproachable. Worship it, admire it, fear it, but keep your distance. There is usually no clear-cut explanation for what it is that is taboo to a tribe, but the two basic laws of totemism are 'not to kill the totem animal and to avoid sexual intercourse with members of the totem clan of the opposite sex' (Freud 1912–13: 85).

The Rat Man similarly created taboos for himself. His strange rules of behaviour, like those of Freud's 'primitive' people, initially appeared to have no rhyme or reason. But, as we remember, Freud found that the Rat Man's obsessive-compulsive beliefs could be traced back to emotional ambivalence, most powerfully to his ambivalence towards his father, who denied him his Oedipal desires and whom he saw as getting in the way of his attempts to love women. In *Totem and Taboo* Freud traces out a logic that connects these animal taboos with the incest taboo and with modern forms of neurotic disease. Yet he also points out a central difference between tribal taboos and obsessive illness. Taboo is a public social structure, while neurosis is a private disease. Taboo structures and organises society, while neurosis makes it difficult to function in society. By comparing the two Freud suggests that a modern social structure, such as organised religion, may also resemble a mass, shared, social neurosis.

One of the Rat Man's most disturbing beliefs was that his father might still appear on his doorstep and judge him, despite the fact that he had been dead for years. In his anthropological work Freud looks at this ancient religious belief in the return of the spirits of the dead. He finds some interesting similarities between them and the ways in which his patients continued to be 'haunted' by their dead, but still powerful, parents. Tribes often had taboos on the dead – people were forbidden to speak the name of a dead relative or friend, or to touch the body; often there were special religious rites that had to be followed about disposing of the body. If these strictures were disregarded the dead would return as furious, haunting demons. Freud sees this fear of the demonic return of the dead as related to the survivors' complicated and guilt-ridden feelings towards the dead:

> When a wife has lost a husband or a daughter her mother, it not infrequently happens that the survivor is overwhelmed by tormenting doubts (to which we give the name of 'obsessive self-reproaches') as to whether she may not herself have been responsible for the death of this cherished being through some act of carelessness or neglect.

> (Freud 1912–13: 116)

These self-reproaches come about because of a conflict that arises between mourning and a secret sense of satisfaction. The mourner's sense of guilt and self-blame emerges from the fact that the mourned object was both loved and hated. This process of conflict is dealt with by the psychical mechanism known in psychoanalytic terminology as projection. In projection:

> The hostility, of which the survivors know nothing and moreover wish to know nothing, is ejected from internal perception into the external world, and thus detached from them and pushed on to someone else.
>
> (Freud 1912–13: 119)

When the dead who we think we simply loved appear to return as ghosts, it is because we have projected our hostility on to them. Our own hostility gets turned around, projected on to the outside world as being directed *towards* us, rather than emerging *from* us. The dead, therefore, appear threatening – returning malevolently to haunt our lives. The self-reproaches that Freud associates with the conscience are also associated with this turning-round of emotion, our need to repress hostile feelings and replace them with positive ones: 'Conscience is the internal perception of the rejection of a particular wish operating within us' (Freud 1912–13: 124).

The third essay in *Totem and Taboo*, 'Animism, Magic and the Omnipotence of Thoughts', begins with the concept of animism, the idea that the world is inhabited by numerous spirits. In animism, animals, plants and people are all seen as animated by a 'soul'. Examining early forms of religious belief, Freud finds they share several traits with the beliefs of neurotics. Believers in animism and neurotics imagine that the power of the mind to create and change the outside world is very strong; they both have faith in imitative magic, the idea that 'If I wish it to rain, I have only to do something that looks like rain or is reminiscent of rain' (Freud 1912–13: 138). According to Freud, belief in certain types of magic replaces the laws of nature by psychological laws. Animated, personified figures become extraordinarily controlling of those they rule over and the world around them. Delusions of persecution in the most extreme forms of psychosis resemble tribal peoples' fear of their deities, who are invested with enormous powers.

Freud, for whom the model of Oedipus is always present, sees paranoiacs' fears as based on an image of a punishing father:

> A son's picture of his father is habitually clothed with excessive powers of this kind, and it is found that distrust of the father is intimately linked with admiration for him. When a paranoiac turns the figure of one of his associates into a 'persecutor', he is raising him to the rank of a father: he is putting him into a position in which he can blame him for all his misfortunes.
>
> (Freud 1912–13: 105)

The totem animal, and the ambivalence that is manifested towards it, resembles this complex of feelings towards the father. The totem animal is both worshipped and sacrificed; it is seen as untouchable, yet eventually, in a sacred ceremony, it is ingested so that its traits can be absorbed into the self of the believer. These ambivalent dynamics of love and awe, combined with hatred and fear, maintaining a safe distance from the object yet also killing and devouring it violently, display all the key emotions that psychoanalysis finds so prevalent in the childhood passions it explores.

What Freud does finally in the last section of *Totem and Taboo*, 'The Return of Totemism in Childhood', is imagine a prehistoric story of the early childhood of mankind to explain the origin of the ambivalent combination of emotions and rituals he finds so central both to primitive religions and to the fears and obsessive practices of neurotics and psychotics. Freud picks up on an idea of Darwin's that primitive man had once lived in hordes in which one male ruled over the pack, having many wives and children. Based on a model of what was currently believed about some species of ape, Freud suggested that the other male tribe members were forced out of the tribe in order to find mates, since the powerful father figure of the tribe had the monopoly on access to all the females. This expulsion of the younger males worked to prevent incest; it also created enormous amounts of resentment and hatred towards the powerful father figure. Freud imagines the following scenario:

> One day the brothers who had been driven out came together, killed and devoured their father and so made an end of the patriarchal horde. United, they had the courage to do, and succeeded in doing, what would have been impossible for them individually … The violent primal father had doubtless been the feared and envied model of each one of the company of brothers: and in the act of devouring him they accomplished their identification with him, and each one of them acquired a portion of his strength.
>
> (Freud 1912–13: 203)

The sons who had killed and eaten their father in this act of rebellion were then consumed by guilt at what they had done; they remembered that they had loved, as well as hated, the father. They found that the father's influence and power seemed to persist after his death; that in fact the image of the dead father was more powerful than the threats of the live one had been. The primal horde found themselves compelled by their guilt and fear to install the father as a god figure. As a group they renounced the right to sexual congress with the women (the wives of the father or, in this version of the myth, their own mothers) who had provoked their insurgence. They also installed the prohibition against eating the totem animal (except on the one ritual occasion a year when they re-enacted the group murder of the father by devouring the totem).

The myth of the origin of the sense of guilt, and the social bond (when the brothers band together they begin to construct the rudiments of community) that Freud creates in *Totem and Taboo*, are in reality the Oedipus complex writ large over a prehistory that appears infantile, instead of just over the childhood of the individual. In *Totem and Taboo* Freud maintains that this primal slaughter of the father was an actual event that really occurred in prehistoric times, the psychic consequence of which haunts us still. However, modern anthropological data contradict the theories that Freud employed as his initial sources. They show no evidence that early humans or pre-human primates were ever organised so as to be dominated by a single male. Working with inaccurate data, Freud creates a fantasy story, but a compelling one. He uses the story to explain the ways in which the repression and control of ambivalent feelings bring individuals together into a social structure. In Freud's myth the band of brothers create a social structure by taking part in a primitive contract, an agreement that none of them will take the father's place and that all of them will worship the image of the dead father.

In the works in which Freud analyses religion and civilisation, his emphasis on the desire for and fear of father figures returns again and again:

> Society was now based on complicity in the common crime; religion was based on the sense of guilt and remorse attaching to it; while morality was based partly on the exigencies of this society and partly on the penance demanded by the sense of guilt.

(Freud 1912–13: 208)

Later, when Freud arrives at his theory of the super-ego, it is another version of this internalised punishing father. According to Freud, Christianity and Judaism are, as we shall see, religions of the father. Not coincidentally, all religion appears in Freud's writings on culture as a staggeringly successful, guilt-inducing, repressive structure – a building block of society, culture and, inevitably, guilt.

RELIGION, SUBLIMATION, SOCIETY: 'THE FUTURE OF AN ILLUSION' (1927) AND 'CIVILIZATION AND ITS DISCONTENTS' (1930)

Freud was no friend to the religious impulse in human beings. Despite the fact that I have often portrayed him in this volume as a myth-maker, he saw himself as an unraveller of myths rather than a creator of them. Placing his faith in reason and scientific analysis, Freud felt that the only way for society to progress was to recognise and acknowledge its libidinal and aggressive impulses. He believed that civilisation – the sum total of all our complicated structures of culture, law, religion and society – arose through the learned repression of individual instinctual urges. Paradoxically, 'every individual is virtually an enemy of civilisation, though civilisation is supposed to be an object of universal human interest' (Freud 1927a: 184). Individual desires are always at odds with the regulations, institutions and laws of society which force them to heel.

In his later writings on society and religion Freud returns to the basic structure he has set in place in *Totem and Taboo*. The sense of guilt which attaches to a Christian concept such as original sin – one in which the individual shares in the guilt of primal ancestors such as Adam and Eve – resembles that structure of the primal murder which posits an ancient crime against an ancient father figure. Even if we do, for one moment, imagine that this murder may have actually taken place, then obviously no one now living actually participated in it. And yet the guilt structure remains; our responsibility is unconscious and buried deep. It attaches as much to crimes we do not commit as to crimes we do. The strictures of conscience work themselves tortuously into our psyches by ingraining a long list of prohibitions and moral imperatives which keep us morally and legally in line.

Freud theorises that religious faith offers mankind a combination of promised protection and threatened punishment. Religion, Freud suggests, is in fact a wish-fulfilling illusion. In a rational society it ought to be given up as superstition, and yet Freud sees no chance of this happening in the near future. Humanity is too dependent on its superstitions – that sense of absolute values that religion promises. The human need for religion, in Freud's opinion, originates in the helplessness of childhood. The first and most powerful figures for the baby, the parents, are recreated through religion in the figure of a simultaneously sheltering and punishing deity. As usual, Freud stresses the importance of the father rather than the mother:

> The derivation of religious needs from the infant's helplessness and the long-ing for the father seems to me incontrovertible, especially since the feeling is not simply prolonged from childhood days, but is permanently sustained by fear of the superior power of Fate. I cannot think of any need in childhood as strong as the need for a father's protection.

(Freud 1930: 72)

Although Freud believes that religion undermines the value of individual life and fixes people in a state of psychic infantilism, he rather glumly concludes that mankind is not yet ready to give up its need for religious belief (Freud 1930: 273). Religion resembles neurotic illness, but therefore also takes its place; religion paradoxically keeps people healthy by making them subscribe to a group neurosis. Many of Freud's beliefs about society and religion show the ways in which mass delusions such as religion replace individual delusions in civilised society.

Religion is 'a store of ideas ... born from man's need to make his helplessness tolerable and built up from the material or memories of the helplessness of his own childhood and the childhood of the human race' (Freud 1927a: 198). Helplessness and desperate need are not the happiest bases for conscience and a sense of responsibility towards others. If conscience was based on repression, as Freud believed, it was a tool of submission rather than a forward-looking, progressive agency. In Freud's account the civilised 'moral' human being is obviously a repressive formation. People are, in reality, bubbling cauldrons of violent and sexual desires waiting to boil over. Civilisation is imagined as holding back, rather than moving forward.

In 'The Future of an Illusion' (1927) Freud damningly critiques the urge towards religious faith, analysing it in terms of a projection out-ward of the super-ego. And, as we have seen earlier, the super-ego is itself a projection inwards of a punishing, castrating father figure. Religious beliefs are 'illusions, fulfilments of the oldest, strongest and most urgent wishes of mankind' (Freud 1927a: 212). But still religion is central to civilisation as Freud imagines it.

In 'Civilization and its Discontents' (1930) Freud draws out his thoughts on religion to encompass many other social structures. Civi-lisation, he argues, emerges initially from humanity's need to conquer the earth, to make its harsh surroundings bearable and serviceable to mankind's needs and desires: '"civilization" [*Kultur* in German] describes the whole sum of the achievements and regulations which distinguish our lives from those of our animal ancestors and which serve two purposes – namely to protect men against nature and to adjust their mutual relations' (Freud 1930: 278). Humanity, at first a feeble animal, has, by the development of its superior brain power, survived and conquered. Of course this process required co-operation; an ability to put aside individual interests and demands in order to maintain an orderly society, apart from a brutal law of kill or be killed. According to Freud, the 'replacement of the power of the individual by the power of a community constitutes the decisive step of civilization' (Freud 1930: 284).

But this step is not an easy or satisfying one for the individual to take. Freud emphasises the ways in which civilisation is built upon repression and **sublimation**.

SUBLIMATION

Sublimation is the process by which instinctual urges and energies get translated into non-instinctual behaviour: 'This capacity to exchange its originally sexual aim for another one, which is no longer sexual but which is psychically related to the first aim, is called the capacity for *sublimation*' (Freud 1908b: 39). For instance, a fascination with the anal stage of development can turn someone into a miser who hoards their money. But sublimation is also imagined as a positive force; it creates art, literature, culture, etc. Civilisation, as a step beyond the meeting of the basic requirements for survival – food and shelter – is based on the process of sublimation. Every monument to civilisation that mankind has created begins, according to Freud, with the need to re-route instinctual energies: 'Sublimation of instinct is an especially conspicuous feature of cultural development; it is what makes it possible for higher psychical activities, scientific, artistic or ideological, to play such an important part in civilized life' (Freud 1930: 286).

In 'Civilization and its Discontents' Freud asks a deceptively simple question – why isn't humanity happy? Is it possible to be happy? He argues that suffering emerges from three main sources for people: 'the superior powers of nature, the feebleness of our own bodies and the inadequacy of regulations which adjust the mutual relationships of human beings in the family, the state and society' (Freud 1930: 274). Mankind has had stunning successes in negotiating the problems created by the first two categories, but the third, the nature of our relations with each other individually or in groups, provides unending sources of pain and dissatisfaction. The individual always seems to suffer in the face of civilised demands. But why is this so?

According to Freud, neurosis appears because of the amount of frustration society imposes upon the individual. There is a built-in antagonism between the demands of the instincts and the repressive structures of society. We suffer as people from external restrictions (for instance, laws and regulations which tell us not to kill our father or sleep with our mother) and internal restrictions (which often keep us from committing those acts even if we knew we would not get caught, because we would feel unbearable guilt if we did). Freud writes that his aim in the essay, which winds up being largely about guilt, is to 'represent the sense of guilt as the most important problem in the development of civilization' (Freud 1930: 327). An advanced civilisation, based on guilt, makes the achievement of happiness extraordinarily difficult.

For the proper achievement of civilisation, Freud maintains, it is necessary to take part in a contractual exchange, even if we don't realise it, even if we feel we have never signed the papers. The group's needs will always be different from the individual's desires; therefore the desires of the individual must give way: 'This replacement of the power of the individual by the power of a community constitutes the decisive step of civilization' (Freud 1930: 284). The legal system exemplifies this requirement. To achieve a level of 'justice for all' there must be guarantees that a law, once made, applies to everyone: it will not be broken to favour an individual. For communities to survive and flourish in the advanced way the structure of society now requires, people must give up a good deal of their personal and sexual freedom. Like the baby who learns from the reality principle that wishes cannot always be satisfied instantaneously, humans – inextricably bound into the contract of civilisation – are forced to learn the same harsh lesson. They sacrifice the idea of instant gratification for the hope of some future good, usually for their own person but, in some altruistic people, for the good of their community or humanity as a whole. These altruistic people, Freud maintains, have achieved a high and gratifying level of sublimation.

Some of Freud's cleverest rhetorical techniques in 'Civilization and its Discontents' are used in the service of disputing the logic of received religious morality. He takes religious commonplaces and dissects them to see where and how they contradict common sense. A central demand of a civil and religious society for Freud is one of Christianity's proudest claims, 'Love thy neighbour as thyself'. Freud suggests that we adopt a naive attitude in trying to understand this command and see if we can make any sense of it. On the one hand, he asks 'Why should we do this?' and, on the other, he asks 'Is it even possible?' What if my neighbour is hostile and vicious towards me – how can it make sense to love him? And then, doesn't it devalue my love to spread it so thinly – shouldn't I reserve my love for those who prove they deserve it? Freud shows the way in which that relationship of neighbour suggests an encroaching aggressiveness. The neighbour seems uncomfortably close to a person without being bound by a tie of blood. The neighbour is not family but not far enough away for us to ignore. And, as we well know, just because someone is family there is no guarantee that, in the psychoanalytic world of emotions, you will treat them to your unqualified love. As we have seen, a mixture of love and hate characterises even the closest relationships. Why should an unknown neighbour fare better than a mother or father? The 'natural' reaction to the neighbour that Freud imagines is aggression, not love:

> men are not gentle creatures who want to be loved, and who, at the most, can defend themselves if they are attacked; they are, on the contrary, creatures among whose instinctual endowments is to be reckoned a powerful share of aggressiveness.

(Freud 1930: 302)

For civilisation to function, everyone is expected to hold back these aggressive instincts. For communities to survive, there must be a universal renunciation of instinctual gratification – but, of course, this renunciation is never universal: there will always be law-breakers, people who gratify their desires as they arise. Freud points out that in relation to the super-ego these are the people who suffer least from its strictures. The individual who is the most moral and who lives life closest to impossible demands such as 'Love thy neighbour as thyself' is actually more likely to suffer from an acute sense of guilt. For the person who commits repeated criminal and antisocial acts must have a super-ego which is not highly developed. A person with a highly developed and punitive super-ego will be suffused with guilt whether or not they have done anything wrong. The psyche is not logical in Freud – it does not dispense punishments or rewards according to who deserves them. In the realm of mental illness it is often the obsessives and neurotics, who are constantly punishing themselves, who have the most acute sense of duty and responsibility towards others. It is the conflicting demands of civilisation and individual desire which make for the repressive ties that bind.

Freud finally offers no solution in 'Civilization and its Discontents' to the problems of the renunciation of instinct that civilised society requires and the lack of individual happiness it can guarantee. It is a speculative and engrossing piece which displays Freud at his most pessimistic. As opposed to the example of Marxism, for instance, psychoanalytic thinking about civilisation sees an inevitable element of aggression and destructiveness built into the human animal. A Marxist would argue that aggression and war can be explained by inequalities in the distribution of wealth. If wealth were distributed equally, aggression would become unnecessary. Humans could get along peacefully because society could fulfil everyone's needs; everyone could get what they want. But psychoanalysis suggests that getting what one wants is a psychic problem as well as a material one. Getting what one wants as a solution to a problem implies, first, knowing what one wants and, second, the assumption that all wishes can be satisfied. Contrary to Marxism (which sees the economic basis of society as determining the individual's inner self), psychoanalysis posits that lack will always signify more than the lack of material possessions to the individual, and that envy, wanting, jealousy and aggression are primal urges and not created by the lack of real material goods. Freud writes:

> One would think that a reordering of human relations should be possible, which would remove the sources of dissatisfaction with civilization by renouncing coercion and the suppression of instincts, so that, undisturbed by internal discord, men might devote themselves to the acquisition of wealth and its enjoyment. That would be the golden age, but it is questionable if such a state of affairs can be realized. It seems rather that every civilization must be built up

> on coercion and renunciation of instinct … One has, I think to reckon with the fact that there are present in all men destructive, and therefore anti-social and anti-cultural, trends and that in a great number of people these are strong enough to determine their behaviour in human society.
>
> (Freud 1930: 185)

'Reckoning' with this fact is left up to the reader at the end of 'Civilization and its Discontents'. There is no obvious way out of the impasse that repressive civilisation seems to imply for Freud.

Freud's writings about culture work primarily to debunk belief, not to provide solutions to the problems of social relations. The psychoanalytic cures he tries to provide at an individual level – the working through and analysis of the symptoms of individual illness through psychoanalytic practice – are difficult to translate to the mass level. For instance, Freud sees religion as filling a need which it would be better for society not to have. But because this need is associated with the most primal desires and fears of childhood – desire for safety and fear of abandonment or punishment – it is hard to imagine how this need might be overcome.

Freud's critique of civilisation in his writings on culture and religion is not done in the name of something higher. He provides no prescription to cure civilised society of what ails it. Despite Freud's reliance on dodgy anthropological ideas about 'primitive' people, psychoanalysis works primarily to dispute the idea that there are 'naturally' degenerate people, races or classes; it breaks down the idea that the pathological is immoral, seeing the pathological as in continuum with the complex, passionate but unquestionably normal state of human emotional life.

In this way Freud questions assumptions about the 'abnormality' of pathological behaviour and desires when he writes about culture as well as when he writes about individuals. In *Totem and Taboo* he imagines that society suffers from a traumatic founding story – a primal murder of a loved and envied father figure that instilled simultaneously the sense of guilt and the need to worship a leader or god. By tracing out the similarities between neuroses, tribal religious practices and infantile beliefs he creates a layered picture of the mind. Buried underneath a surface of civilised, rational, scientific belief there is a sense in which we all still have faith in magic, in the power of thought to kill or wound, in the power of repeated ritual to affect the outside world. Freud lived in fear that psychoanalysis would be seen (as it often was) as an alternative religion. He wanted his own ideas to be firmly on the side of science. But then again he also often acted like a religious leader; he demanded absolute loyalty from his followers; he insisted that true analysts would never stray far from his ideas of the central tenets of psychoanalysis. One might argue that Freud, too, fell victim to that intractable human desire for faith in something higher – a substitute god or father figure. In a sense he set up himself and psychoanalysis as that father.

As social theory, psychoanalysis can appear quite conservative. Freud does not have much faith in social utopias such as the one that communism promises. His view of human nature is pessimistic and sceptical – he doesn't believe that a shift in economic factors could change the basic nature of humanity. Freud appears to accept society's norms at the same time as recognising that they are not natural or written in stone. Rather, society's norms are viewed as repressive but often necessary. All psychoanalysis can offer in this instance is a new way of understanding them. Psychoanalysis, in this sense, supports the *status quo*. It is not a theory of individual or social transformation. Human nature (the id) is intractable in its desires.

SUMMARY

Freud's ideas about anthropology are now viewed as based on mistaken assumptions about 'primitive' peoples and human prehistory. Yet his conclusions are none the less often psychologically intriguing. In his writings on religion, society and anthropology Freud sees similarities between religious ritual and the pathological practices of obsessive-compulsives and neurotics. In *Totem and Taboo* he creates an Oedipal myth to explain the origins of society – one in which a tribal band of brothers joins together to overthrow and kill the leader of their tribe and the father of them all, thus gaining access to the forbidden females of the horde. In 'The Future of an Illusion' and 'Civilization and its Discontents' Freud puts forward the thesis that the source of both religious practices and the practices of civilised society is the repression of instinctual urges. Civilisation as we know it exists because humans are capable of the process of sublimation, the process by which instinctual urges – demands for sex, food, the death of enemies – are changed into non-instinctual behaviour – such as politics, art and music, but also neurotic illness. Freud's ideas on civilisation lead us to the conclusion that we are all potentially monsters in the unconscious; it is just that the repressive restrictions of civilisation prevent most of us from acting on our desires. According to Freud, the childhood of the individual as well as the childhood of the race survive in the depths of the individual mind, and it is not clear that civilisation can provide a satisfying alternative to those early desires and demands. Instead, our civilisation and religion often leave humankind unsatisfied, wanting more happiness but unable to achieve it. Civilisation is, in a sense, primarily a mode of keeping unruly desires reined in and usefully sublimated into the potential pleasures of culture. We will now turn to the ways in which psychoanalytic thinking has been adopted for interpreting these pleasures, particularly those of art and literature, and why, especially in recent days, psychoanalysis has provoked both gleeful agreement and enormous resistance. We return once again to the question of my opening chapter, Why Freud? and add, Why now?

AFTER FREUD

Like an endlessly recyclable horror-film axe murderer, the more psychoanalysis is killed off the more it comes back to haunt our culture. This would be no surprise to Freud himself, who insisted that the repressed always returns. The onslaught of attacks on Freud, the renewed emphasis on the biological causes of mental illness, and a turn toward explanations of human behaviour based in evolutionary psychology is turning psychoanalysis into the repressed of our day and age. Therefore, from the psychoanalytic perspective, we can expect it to return spectacularly. One of the most prominent forms of its recent return has been in the area of literary theory. In this concluding chapter we will look at how, over the last century, psychoanalysis has mutated from being a specialised and much disputed view of the mind into, amongst other things, an influential method of understanding modern literature and culture. Psychoanalytic theory has been particularly effective in the area of literary and film criticism, its reading techniques widely disseminated, even when they are not always labelled psychoanalytic. As we saw in the last chapter, Freud was always eager to extend the domain of psychoanalytic insight into vast new arenas. In this final chapter we will examine the ways in which this has taken place beyond Freud.

When thinking 'beyond' Freud it is important to remember that the terms Freudian and psychoanalytic are not entirely substitutable for one another. From the beginning many of Freud's followers dissented from some of his ideas and formulated their own versions of psychoanalysis which disagreed with one or more of Freud's premises. Here I will only mention, in passing, Melanie Klein (1882–1960), an important analyst who followed Freud and whose ideas have been taken up by literary scholars as well as psychoanalysts. Klein saw herself as elaborating on and extending Freud's original theories, but she also changed his emphases. Unlike Freud, Klein worked directly with children, finding aggressive fantasies of murderous rage and envy in the very young. She too posited a version of the death drive, and her work with very young children suggested that there were psychic dramas of development that extended even further into infancy than Freud was willing to go. If Freud focused primarily on the Oedipal crisis and the entry of the father into the child's world, Klein was more interested in the loves, hates and wants of the pre-Oedipal, non-verbal child and his or her intense relationship with the mother. Klein developed the technique of play therapy, which assumed that the ways in which children drew or played with toys could reveal underlying fantasies and anxieties, even if they were too young to verbalise their fears. She also founded Object Relations theory. Freud had introduced the idea of object choice; at different times during the infant's development one or other parent is the object of the baby's need and desire. Klein became interested in the ways in which a parental figure could become objectified even further, so that a part of the parental body such as the breast could play an important role in infantile development as the object of love, rage or anxiety about its possible withdrawal. Klein's ideas about play and object relations offer a way of thinking through the baby's early relations with the mother which has been seen by some feminist critics as an important corrective to Freud's focus on the Oedipal father and the masculine child (See Klein 1985; Rose 1993; Jacobus 2005; Phillips and Stonebridge 1998.) Although this book is focused on Freud, his ideas and his impact on literary and cultural criticism, it is worth remembering that other versions of psychoanalysis have also left their mark.

Freud's ideas have always provoked controversy and discussion within the confines of the analytic community and outside it. At the end of this discussion we will consider the many strong reactions psychoanalysis has inspired – the hatred and the love, the faith and the mistrust. Freud's personal life, his analytic practice and his theories of sexuality have provoked enormous heated debate. One of the most important recent critiques emerged initially from the feminist movement in the 1970s. Since then the feminist critique of Freud has been supplemented by many others in what some have seen as a demolition job. We are forced at the end of this book devoted to explicating Freud's ideas to return with more force to our initial question: 'Why Freud?'

FREUD'S WRITINGS ON ART AND LITERATURE

As with his attempts to annex religion and society as objects upon which psychoanalysis could usefully comment, Freud also found himself drawn towards the psychoanalytic analysis of art and literature. Richard Wollheim points out that Freud's writings on art usually focus on the psychology of the artists, rather than on analyses of particular paintings or stories (Wollheim 1991: 252). Freud's essays on Leonardo da Vinci and Dostoevsky, 'Leonardo da Vinci and a Memory of his Childhood' (1910) and 'Dostoevsky and Parricide' (1928), are psychoanalytic biographies; they comment on the artist, not the work of art itself. This brings us to a key question: can there be a psychoanalytic analysis without a human being who has memories, a childhood, desires on which to base a reading? What would it mean to have a psychoanalytic reading that was not of a person, but of a text? Psychoanalytically inclined literary critics post-Freud make these questions central to their project. I shall return to them in the next section of this chapter.

For Freud himself, and for his early followers, reading an artwork psychoanalytically usually involved delving into the artist's conscious and unconscious motivations for the work. In his article 'Creative Writers and Day-dreaming' (1908) Freud compares the artist's work to child's play: 'Might we not say that every child at play behaves like a creative writer, in that he creates a world of his own, or, rather, rearranges the things of his world in a new way which pleases him?' (Freud 1908a: 131–2). As we grow up this early period of play turns into the daydreams that we all indulge in during any given day. According to Freud, daydreams, like play, and the dreams of the night are geared primarily towards fulfilling wishes that we cannot fulfil in real life. In these wishes the unconscious roams free, satisfying in fantasy what is more difficult to satisfy in the real world. Fantasising is the adult equivalent of play, the residue of these childhood pleasures which we are loath to leave behind. If a person is talented enough at fantasising and converting those fantasies into artistic form, he or she may become an artist.

Freud believed that the source of artistic creativity was the same as the source of all other formations of civilisation: sublimated instincts. (See Chapter 6 for definition of sublimation, p. 103.) As we saw in the last chapter, society as a whole is based on repression; in the course of everyday lives we all learn to repress. Some people do this more easily than others, however. If you remember, the effort of keeping neurotics' desires and urges under psychic wraps consequently made them ill. By contrast, artists find a more creative outlet for these potentially neurosis-causing desires. According to Freud, great artists take their infantile sexual urges and successfully sublimate them into their work. As Freud was aware, this does not in any sense explain the source of artistic talent or genius – we all daydream, we all play childhood games, but very few of us create the works of Leonardo da Vinci or Dostoevsky. Freud did not pretend to explain the mechanism by which one person's sublimations were considered beautiful and another's the ravings of a madman, but these questions hover in the background of Freud's assumptions about the relationship between art and repression.

One drawback of Freud's explanations is that they seem to lump artistic genius and neurosis together; both indicate an inability to deal with reality, a regression to childhood urges and desires. The artist differs from the neurotic only in so far as he has the talent to make his regressive tendencies pay. This assumption winds up binding talent and neurotic illness together in the figure of the 'mad genius'. The early part of the twentieth century saw a series of 'pathographies' written by psychoanalysts and other psychologists, studies of particular artists that analysed their creations according to their pathological complexes; many early psychoanalytic writings on art and literature fell into this category (Wright 1984: 34). By ignoring the artistic status of a work of art – its form, rhyme scheme, dramatic structure, etc. – pathography leads to limited and unsatisfying psychoanalytic readings. Freud sometimes employs this method for deducing the childhood neuroses of artists, but he was not entirely convinced of it.

When Freud does not speculate about the early instinctual motives of the artist – for instance, Leonardo's homosexuality and attachment to his mother ('Leonardo da Vinci and a Memory of his Childhood', 1910) – he usually analyses the content of various short stories, myths, novels and plays. He often uses literary sources to provide supporting evidence for his theories, most famously in his citation of *Oedipus the King* and *Hamlet* to support his ideas about the Oedipal crisis (see Chapter 3 for *Oedipus*). Freud the literary critic acts like Freud the analyst (and, for that matter, Freud the detective): he combs the texts carefully to uncover motivations that make the characters in the book behave as they do. He often finds these motivating factors, once again, buried in the characters' pasts.

To take an example from *The Interpretation of Dreams*: Freud asks why is it that, at a crucial moment in the play, Hamlet is unable to avenge his father's death by killing his uncle Claudius, even though he is given the perfect opportunity to do so? According to Freud's Oedipal reading of the play, Hamlet's hesitation is based on the fact that he too closely identifies with the man he is required to kill. Claudius, who has murdered Hamlet's father and married his mother, has simply acted out Hamlet's own Oedipal desires:

> Hamlet is able to do anything – except take vengeance on the man who did away with his father and took that father's place with his mother, the man who shows him the repressed wishes of his own childhood realised. Thus the loathing that should drive him on to revenge is replaced in him by self-reproaches, by scruples of conscience, which remind him that he himself is literally no better than the sinner whom he is to punish.
>
> (Freud 1900: 367)

This interpretation relies on certain assumptions that we might want to examine more closely. Here Freud shifts from analysing the character and motivations of the *author* of a work to analysing the personality and motivations of a *character* in a book or play. Yet similar objections to his methods still arise. How, we might well ask, can we interpret the motives of a character in a book as related to his or her childhood fantasies and desires when we know in fact that the character is simply an invention of the author and never had a 'real' childhood at all? Characters in novels do not have a store of traumatic memories to draw upon; they do not dream unless those dreams are explicitly described in their stories; they do not witness primal scenes of their parents having sex unless that event is included in the book itself. If there is an unconscious at play in the reading of a text, the word must have a meaning very different from the one it carries when applied to an individual human being. This is a problem we will return to in the psychoanalytic literary criticism section of this chapter, but for the moment let us examine closely an example of Freud's methods when he analyses literary work.

'THE "UNCANNY"' (1919)

Some of Freud's most interesting speculations on literature emerge when he avoids the two previously discussed psychoanalytic approaches to art – treating invented characters as real people with real pasts that can be analysed, or assuming that one can understand a work of art fully by analysing the author's childhood sexual fantasies, psychic motivations, etc. In his article 'The "Uncanny"' he explores a single concept as it threads its way through literature and life. 'The "Uncanny"' mixes together insightful speculation and occasionally heavy-handed readings. In this article Freud devotes himself to uncovering the meanings of an aesthetic concept – the feeling of the 'uncanny'. He discusses the term uncanny (in German, *unheimlich*) as a specific form of frightening phenomenon that we find in literature and in life. When we encounter the uncanny we are left feeling spooked and, perhaps, uncertain of the exact source of that fear. What strikes people as frightening, however, varies from person to person. In the article, Freud attempts to find a common thread amongst the differing forms of the uncanny. He traces the changing meanings of *unheimlich* and he also analyses a number of literary works that he considers uncanny. He comes to the following conclusion about what unites all these experiences: 'the uncanny is that class of the frightening which leads back to what is known of old and long familiar' (Freud 1919: 340).

Freud arrived at this conclusion originally by trawling through a German dictionary to discover the history of the word *heimlich*. *Heimlich*'s original meaning was 'of the house', familiar, intimate, or friendly. As Freud traces its origins he discovers it has come to mean something else entirely, namely secret or concealed – the opposite of familiar: 'Thus *heimlich* is a word the meaning of which develops in the direction of ambivalence, until it finally coincides with its opposite, *unheimlich*' (Freud 1919: 347). Why, Freud asks, is there this doubling of contradictory meanings?

Freud attempts to answer this question by analysing various examples of the uncanny, spending a large section of the article on the German author E.T.A. Hoffmann's strange story 'The Sandman'. Without going into all the details of Freud's complicated reading, I will emphasise the one he also chooses to stress. Freud interprets a particular scene involving a little boy's fears of losing his eyes as necessarily symbolising castration. This is one of those moments where Freud appears to be reading like a crude Freudian, using a heavy symbolic and sexual interpretation to uncover the one true (sexual) meaning of the story. (See Chapter 2 for more on Freudian sexual symbolism and its 'crude' uses.) In fact the alternative sources of uncanny feeling that Freud discusses in other parts of the article are rich and wide-ranging.

We might suspect that death would be a more natural source of the uncanny then sexuality, and Freud initially appears to agree: 'Many people experience the feeling in the highest degree in relation to death and dead bodies, to the return of the dead, and to spirits and ghosts' (Freud 1919: 364). The sense of the uncanny is also very much connected with fears of doubles, especially the fear of oneself having a double. Freud claims that this too relates to primitive beliefs about death. He writes, referring to another analyst Otto Rank's 1914 book on *The Double*, that the double in ancient religion or folklore was 'originally an insurance against the destruction of the ego, an "energetic denial of the power of death", as Rank says; and probably the "immortal" soul was the first "double" of the body' (Freud 1919: 356). Images of the dead were, according to Freud, originally meant to preserve a continuity between life and death, suggesting that the soul would live on. However, at some point the double reversed itself and became, instead of protection against death, a forewarning of its imminent approach.

The uncanny for Freud, and the ambivalent nature of its two meanings – familiar and unfamiliar – is inseparable from the repeated return of the repressed. A familiar word, if it is repeated too often, can begin to seem unfamiliar; ancient beliefs which were meant to comfort humans for the transience of life can turn into fear of the dead. One of Freud's examples shows brilliantly how he ties this fear of the dead back into the special hobby-horse psychoanalysis, the fears and anxieties surrounding sexuality:

> It often happens that neurotic men declare that they feel there is something uncanny about the female genital organs. This *unheimlich* place, however, is the entrance to the former *Heim* [home] of all human beings, to the place where each one of us lived once upon a time and in the beginning ... whenever a man dreams of a place or country and says to himself, while he is still dreaming: 'this place is familiar to me, I've been here before,' we may interpret the place as being his mother's genitals or her body.
>
> (Freud 1919: 368)

Freud's readings such as this show off his creative flair; they can also make him sound like a one-note wonder. Of course that note is sex – the source of all life, but paradoxically, here, also a reminder of death. Home is the womb, and the womb is where we are before our lives as individuals begin; associated with the death of the self, this *heimlich / unheimlich* doubling of ambivalent meanings around the female genitalia returns us, in fantasy, to a former safe, protected but simultaneously deathly and frightening pre-natal state. Freud's theories suggested that children who seek information about their own origin – the question 'Where do babies come from?' – are also forced to confront a potentially frightening fact: the idea that they once did not exist, that before they were themselves human beings, they came originally from the powerful 'nowhere' of their mother's body. (See Chapter 3 for the relation of Oedipus to these questions.) The womb, the earliest home of us all, may logically also seem like a terrifying, deathlike place which pre-dates our own existence.

However, along with the return to the womb, Freud is also concerned with the distinctly literary nature of uncanny effects, situating uncanny feelings on the border between fiction and reality. He writes: 'an uncanny effect is often and easily produced when the distinction between imagination and reality is effaced, as when something that we have hitherto regarded as imaginary appears before us in reality, or when a symbol takes over the full function of the thing it symbolizes' (Freud 1919: 367). This indicates another way in which psychoanalytic criticism is very much bound up with the literary. Psychoanalysis is centrally concerned with the difficulty of maintaining the distinction between imagination and reality. When the superficially fantastical content of our dreams tells us something real about our past and our present; when our earliest fantasised relations with our parents affect how we see ourselves and our lives; then it is clear that this aspect of

the uncanny may be crucial to understanding Freud's central contentions. If psychoanalysis is centrally concerned with how or if we can
negotiate the line between imagination and reality, then it is a very
literary endeavour indeed.

Freud exercises his considerable talents as a literary critic in the
course of 'The "Uncanny"' and finds himself, once again, in the
familiar realm of productive contradiction. On the one hand, he suggests that uncanny feelings may be related to the ways in which we can
never entirely separate the workings of our mind and our 'reality'. He
is fascinated by the ways in which the presumably literary realm – the
world of the imagination as explored by artists, writers, and all of us
in fantasy – impinges upon, affects and shapes our 'real' lives. These
speculations of Freud's stress the inevitability of further interpretation;
the uncanny cannot be securely pinned down as one thing (fantasy) or
another (reality) because perhaps those two are not as separable as we
would like them to be. On the other hand, his symbolic readings of
events in 'The Sandman', or of the human fear of death, inevitably lead
towards the same arena: castration or the womb, the realm of early
instinctive and sexual desires.

These desires, as we have seen, are usually analysed in the same way
whether they are the desires of characters in books or of the authors
of those books. Why, then, if there are limits to the usefulness of
these kinds of psychoanalytic readings of literature, has modern literary criticism found psychoanalysis so compelling? How do later
critics pick up on Freud's ideas and change them so as to avoid the
pitfalls of putting characters or authors on the psychoanalytic couch?

PSYCHOANALYTIC LITERARY CRITICISM AFTER FREUD

As we have seen, Freud's criticism of specific works of art and literature typically examines the psychic motives of either the characters in
the work or the artist him or herself (usually himself). Even when
Freud strayed into other kinds of literary analysis, as he does in his
analysis of the word *unheimlich*, the material that he analysed was
inevitably the *content* of the work (or the content of the artist's life).
Recent theorists who have picked up on the potential of psychoanalysis for literature often focus on the *form* of the work, an area
Freud neglected. To give examples of these two different kinds of

analytic readings – content versus form – I will turn first to the readings of an analytic colleague and friend of Freud's, Marie Bonaparte (1882–1962).

Marie Bonaparte's book-length study of Edgar Allan Poe analyses the life of the troubled author, whose poverty, alcoholism and marriage to his thirteen-year-old cousin made him an ideal candidate for the psychoanalytic tendency to see an artist's work as the reflection of his (neurotic) life. As well as interpreting Poe's stories through his life, Bonaparte analyses many of his morbid tales individually, showing how they reveal a fixation on his dead mother which manifests itself in necrophiliac desires (sexual attraction to the dead). Bonaparte discovers female and male genital symbolism in the dungeons and tombs of Poe's tales; according to Bonaparte, in Poe's famous story 'The Purloined Letter' (in which a stolen letter is eventually discovered by the master detective Dupin in the most obvious place), the letter, which lies hidden in plain sight hanging from a mantelpiece, symbolises the much-coveted penis that hangs between the man's legs. Bonaparte does not attend to the ways in which Poe's stories are told, their narrative structures or rhetorical techniques; hers is an example of content-based psychoanalytic reading. As far as Bonaparte is concerned it matters not at all that Poe wrote short stories and poetry rather than novels or plays. The content – sexual symbolism – remains the same.

A psychoanalytic reading of Poe that focused on form as well as content might take into account that many of Poe's stories are told in the first person; that some of them seem like confessions of crimes; that the rhythm of his poetry affects how the reader or hearer understands it. Sexual symbolism may still enter into a reading that focuses on the form of a work, but the meaning of that sexual symbol will vary in relation to other formal factors of the work. The French analyst Jacques Lacan's 'Seminar on "The Purloined Letter"' differs from Bonaparte's reading in ways which are too complicated to summarise here, but which rely on a structural interpretation of the characters in the story; the ways in which characters take up certain positions of knowledge and ignorance; power and disempowerment, in relation to each other. I will return briefly to the ways in which Lacan's theories reread Freud through the lens of language in the next section of this chapter (also see Lacan 1988: 191–205; Wright 1984: 105–7, Bowie 1991).

Although readings which take the specific forms of literature into account seem preferable to ones that do not, I am not claiming that content-based psychoanalytic readings are necessarily mistaken. Overtly sexual readings of books are an easy target for critical ridicule – when every dagger in *Macbeth* represents a penis, the play can begin to seem a bit predictable. Yet sexual symbolism can also suggest intriguing interpretations of literature. If sexual symbolism is used in isolation, however, without reference to the specific narrative structure or techniques of a story, or the syntax or form of a poem, the chances are that psychoanalytic critics will discover nothing but what they are always expecting to find: representations of the phallus or the return to the womb endlessly multiplied.

What, then, does psychoanalysis have to offer literary criticism, other than this content-based focus on sexual symbolism? Can we do a psychoanalytic interpretation in which the reading of a text does not finally focus on sex – either the sexual problems of the author or the sexual symbolism of the narrative? One way out of this impasse might be to look at other areas of Freud's thought – his interest in the techniques and play of interpretation, for instance. As we discussed in Chapter 3, the techniques and concepts Freud used to interpret people's dreams – free association and dream-work – opened up the possibility that interpretation was an endless process, rather than a riddle with a single solution.

The focus on dream-work and free association also provides another way of thinking differently about what psychoanalysis has to offer literature. If interpretation is a process that does not come to a definite end, it may be that the relationship between a reader and a book resembles the relationship between the analyst and the patient, who engage in the process of transference. This at first glance may seem illogical. If you recall, psychoanalytic transference as defined previously (see p. 38) takes place between two people. In a working analysis the patient will transfer strong emotions that he holds or has held for other people – for instance, his parents – on to the analyst. In a sense, the psychoanalytic office resembles a theatre during transference; the analyst is made to play a role, unconsciously, by the patient, who then responds to the analyst as if he were responding to a person from an earlier period in his life.

Transference suggests that reading or understanding others is always a process which involves an exchange of emotional presuppositions. A simple way of saying this might be that every person brings their old emotional baggage to every new relationship they form – every person's unconscious holds the residues of those earliest relationships with parents and siblings, not to mention old friends and lovers. All relationships are refracted through these earlier moments; as we know, early-childhood expectations and disappointments continue to exist in the unconscious even when they appear to be forgotten.

One goal of analysis is to shift the form in which these early emotions appear, from uncontrolled emotion to well understood narratives of the past. In his article 'Remembering, Repeating and Working Through' Freud describes the movement through the play-acting of transference and out the other side that is a key move towards health for the patient. When patients are caught up in transference – treating the analyst as a parent, for instance – they do not realise that they are doing it. Patients are completely enveloped by the role that they play and the role into which they have put the therapist; they unconsciously repeat scenes from their past life without being able to step outside those repetitions and identify the origins of their strong feelings. The analyst's job is to guide the patient towards the recognition of the play in which both of them are performers. Once patients have remembered the events and emotions that inspired the blockages and repetitions in their lives, once they have begun to construct a narrative which allows them to analyse their actions and emotions rather than just acting them out repetitively, they move to the next stage of analysis – working through. 'The success of the analysis depends upon converting re-enactment into memory: through the "talking cure", the language of remembrance takes the place of the compulsive rehearsals of the past' (Ellmann 1994: 8).

The importance of storytelling and play-acting to the analytic scene becomes clear in this definition of transference. But we are still talking about storytelling and play-acting between two people, not between a person and a work of literature. Transference between people seems to make sense, but how can there be transference between a person and a book? How can one establish a transferential relationship with literature?

Post-structuralist psychoanalytic literary critics have brought the idea of transference to bear on the act of reading by emphasising the portions of Freud's theories which claim that the act of reading is always a process, and never a fully stable one. When we read, the text affects us; our readings affect the text. Post-structuralist criticism has also emphasised that the author's intentions are never fully retrievable from the text we are given (see Barthes 1995). Writing severs itself from the intentions of the author when it appears on a page – we may surmise that we know what that writer meant to communicate, but we can never be completely sure, because, as Freud, along with poets and novelists throughout history, has shown, words always come in multiple, layered meanings. They signify differently in different contexts, and sometimes they signify doubly in the same context (think of the example of *unheimlich*). Furthermore, the delving of psychoanalysis into unconscious motivations and meanings suggests that we could not be sure of the intentions behind a text even if we had the author in the room with us and could ask him or her what he or she meant. The existence of unconscious desires means that our motives can be murky, even (or, as Freudian slips suggest, sometimes especially) to ourselves. So we can see two related arguments here for the impossibility of pinning down a single stable meaning of a literary text. One is that language itself defers meaning – the meanings of words always potentially shift and change. (If, for instance, you look up the meaning of a word in a dictionary to try and pin it down you will invariably find more words, with more meanings that you must look up. There is no foreseeable end to this process.) The other argument is that the existence of unconscious desires also defers the final assignment of meaning: because of the unconscious, a text always means more and differently than what the author intended; we may always be also saying something other than what we think we mean.

In the relationship that emerged in early psychoanalytic criticism of literature, psychoanalysis took the position of interpreting analyst to literature's object of analysis. A story viewed through a psychoanalytic framework would reveal its hidden (often sexual) meanings. But critics such as Shoshona Felman have suggested that this relationship can be reversed; literature may also usefully read psychoanalysis, and inform and critique its suppositions and positions (Felman 1977a). In the first instance this suggests the possibility of subjecting Freud's writings to the same processes of reading that we would apply to a poem or novel. Throughout this book the idea that Freud should be read both critically, to discover the contradictions and fissures in his ideas, and for his rhetoric has been an underlying theme. When we go to the case histories and read 'Dora' as if we were reading a melodramatic novel of the *fin de siècle*, the readings that emerge are different from those that would appear if we viewed Freud's account of Dora as a scientific, objective unfolding of a medical case. We always bring presuppositions to a text (for instance, the expectations we have when we sit down to read a medical study), but our reading of the text is always capable of undermining those presuppositions. This is one sense in which the reader can be seen to participate in a transferential dynamic with a text.

Furthermore, when Freud writes, he is, not surprisingly, interested in convincing readers of his position. He repeatedly uses certain metaphors to help ground his claims – for instance, the comparison between archaeology and psychoanalysis, in which one discovers the past civilisation buried under the present one. (For analyses of Freud's rhetoric see Fish 1988 and Mahony 1987.) In the process of interpreting the evidence around him Freud also constructs a rhetorically powerful way of reading the world. One of the lessons that can be taken from the methods of psychoanalytic interpretation is that the process of reading does not simply involve unearthing what is already there in a text; it also always involves creation or construction. For Anna O., reconstructing her past simultaneously meant constructing it anew, in a way which she could then take control of. On the first page of this book I described Freud as a myth-maker for our culture. One definition of a myth-maker might be one who creates stories that others find compelling, that others see themselves reflected in; stories which, in some sense, both are true and also become true.

Perhaps this brings us closer to an understanding of what transference between literature and psychoanalysis might be. The strength of psychoanalysis as a technique for reading and understanding rests partly on its important recognition of the construction of meaning that goes on in any attempt to tell a story, whether that story is a childhood memory, a scientific theory or a fairy tale. Perhaps the correct question is not 'How is it possible to have transference on to a literary text?' but rather 'How is it possible not to?' When we read, we turn language from dead words on a page – infinitely interpretable but not yet interpreted marks – into meaning-filled objects. We as readers give books new life, but we also read them through the lens of past readings. We could also claim that books read us, that the stories we tell about our 'real' lives are inseparable from the fictions and fictional forms we have read and lived through. We may view our own lives as taking the form of a romantic novel or a medical case study (see, for instance, the Wolf Man's relationship to Freud's famous writing of his life, pp. 65–68). The concept of transference, as laid out by Freud, is a significant aspect of many recent theories of reading, such as reader-response and post-structural psychoanalytic theories. The combination of a post-structuralist focus on the workings of language and the desires unearthed by Freud's stress on the centrality and shifting forms of memory and sexuality plays a key role in the analytic work of the French psychoanalyst Jacques Lacan (1901–81), to whom I shall now turn. But, before I do so, I will first briefly explore the history of the feminist critique of Freud, and the subsequent reclaiming of a different Freud for feminism.

FEMINISM, LACAN AND FILM THEORY

Throughout this book, particularly in the chapters on sexuality and the case histories, it has probably become clear why feminists might have good reason to be dissatisfied with the deductions of psychoanalysis. Freud's views of women are full of ideas which are notoriously difficult to reconcile with a feminist viewpoint. During the 1970s and 1980s (as they had earlier during the 1920s – see Appignanesi and Forrester 1992) women readers of Freud found much to dispute. Centrally, Freud's focus on penis envy suggested that most women viewed themselves as incomplete men: men who were missing something. Freud's focus on the conflicting directions that the Oedipus crisis took for men and women also led him to claim that women's moral development was much weaker then men's: 'for women the level of what is ethically normal is different from what it is in men. Their super-ego is never so inexorable, so impersonal, so independent of its emotional origins as we require it to be in men' (Freud 1925b: 342). Psychoanalytic ideas were also used to claim that women were naturally passive and masochistic. Although the force of many of Freud's early arguments about sexuality was towards a move away from biological determinism, his later articles suggested that psychic determinism – the development of sex and gender difference in the unconscious – was just as inevitable and just as damaging: 'Time and again, psychoanalysis was seen, even by those ... sympathetic to the idea of such a theory, to be not a theory of sexual differences, but a rationalization and legitimation of already existent social roles' (Appi-ganesi and Forrester 1992: 457).

In an early feminist classic, first published in 1949, *The Second Sex*, Simone de Beauvoir argued that psychoanalysis focused entirely on the masculine model of development, placing the boy's penis at the centre of the universe, as *the* desired object, craved by both boys and girls alike (de Beauvoir: [1949] 1992). *The Second Sex* pointed out the ways in which Freud, in his universalising analyses of the structures of psychic fantasy, ignored the social inequalities that contribute to forming the interior life of all boys and girls. In patriarchal societies boys are more valued than girls; they have more social power. If there is such a thing as penis envy in Freud's terms, it would be logical to see it as the little girl's envy of what the penis represents, rather than of the object itself. As Maud Ellmann puts it, 'women have good reason to envy an organ that promises authority and freedom' (Ellmann 1994).

This position can be seen to both detract from and support Freud's theories of sexual difference. On the one hand, it criticises Freud's determinist ideas about women's sexuality for their blindness to the constraining social situations in which women are placed by patriarchal authority. A glance back over Dora's history will easily convince us of Freud's blindness to certain aspects of her case, and his sometimes bullying mishandling of her emotional state. On the other hand, de Beauvoir's theories can also be used to point out the powerful force of Freud's arguments. If we shift Freud's terms slightly, we can say that Freud was right in his analysis of how women experience sexual difference as a loss or lack; however, the loss is not of an organ but of a position (a position which, in fact, they have never been able to occupy). It is not a specific body part but authority, self-confidence, esteem that every-one craves. In our society men appear to have more access to these kinds of social and ego-forming powers than women. Therefore one argument claims that Freud was right about the structure of gender inequality, even if he was terribly wrong about its causes.

The quirky, difficult to read but fascinating French analyst Jacques Lacan took Freud's ideas about the functioning of sexuality and the unconscious and applied those ideas to language, claiming that sexual and gender identity formation always takes place within language. Recall our earlier discussion of the baby at the breast: as infants we begin to realise that we are separate beings in the world only at the moment that our need for food or warmth is not met. At that moment of recognising what we lack, we cry out, enter the realm of language and simultaneously understand ourselves as separate individuals (see Chapter 3, pp. 41–42). This story is very important to Lacan, who links it with the discovery of a gendered identity in language as well. A baby comes to know itself by realising that he or she is an 'I', an ego, and eventually by claiming that 'I' through language. When we say 'I', we also recognise ourselves as having a sex that is inseparable from that 'I' identity. Yet 'I' is an unstable word: what linguistic discourse terms a 'shifter'. 'I' always refers to the person who speaks, but the identity of that person shifts according to who uses the word. The shifting nature of 'I' comes to signify the relational and shifting nature of identity in language, while the sexed position of 'I' is simultaneously an inescapable part of our identity.

Lacan also changed Freud's concept of the centrality of the penis by replacing it with a different term – the phallus. According to Lacan the phallus symbolises something other than the biological male organ. However, Lacan would not agree with de Beauvoir that what it symbolises is simply the socially constructed position of masculine patriarchal power. Rather, the phallus is a signifier for both male and female: it represents a position in language, a position of wholeness and fulfilment that is aspired to by both sexes but unreachable by either. For Lacan, language responds to a universal lack – we learn to symbolise in order to express our sense of missing something that we all need – food, warmth, security. We begin to use language in order to tell our parents that we are no longer complete, no longer one with the world – we indicate to them what is missing in the hope that they may be able to fill the gap.

According to Lacan, this primal sense of loss that forces us into the use of language in the hope of plugging that gap also propels us into recognising ourselves as separate individuals. Through the recognition of loss we come to a sense of our identity within language, as manipulators of language. This sense of identity is always a tragic one, an identity based on a lack that will never be filled. For Lacan, language functions as a sticking-plaster on the gaping psychic wound of primal separation. The phallus, which in the Lacanian schema no one has, promises the possibility of wholeness, completion, perfect knowledge and authority, yet neither men nor women can have the phallus, because it is an unachievable position in language. Since all language is based on lack (we use a word to signify something because we do not necessarily have the thing itself — we say the word 'cat' to communicate a specific meaning, despite the fact that there may not be one in the room), we all live under a regime of unfulfillable desire. Completely satisfied desire, like a whole and complete identity, is a fantasy; in fact it is one of the defining fantasies that psychoanalysis attempts to negotiate. Freud's definition of the unconscious makes a completely self-knowing, unlacking identity inconceivable. Although we can bring to the surface some unconscious desires, the unconscious itself can never be eradicated; there are always aspects of ourselves that remain unfathomable. For Lacan, our sexual and linguistic identities coalesce around this self-ignorance and lack.

Although Lacan himself is very far from feminist, feminist critics have used his ideas to explain the ways in which sexual difference relies on psychic fantasy rather than biological fact. The relationship of both men and women to the phallus is similarly one of lack in the Lacanian symbolic system; it is not that men have in reality what women crave in fantasy. In this sense Lacan's theories have been influential for feminist critics, who see the centrality of the construction of sexual identity in language as a useful way of recognising that sexual difference is a construct, while at the same time recognising that it is a construct which is internal to our very images of ourselves as separate, speaking, sexed individuals (see Mitchell 1974; Mitchell and Rose 1982; Brennan 1989).

Similarly, Lacan's insistence that identity is formed through desire and in language has made him particularly significant for psychoanalytic literary critics. Shoshona Felman's brilliant reading of Henry James's ghost story 'The Turn of the Screw' relies on radical Lacanian concepts of the possibility of transference between reader and text. She looks at the various narrative frames of James's ghost story, which involves the haunting of two children by dead servants from their household. The notion of mastery is a question that is important to how we read the tale and how we read the main figure of the governess — who has been variously interpreted as a heroic figure attempting to save the children from demonic influences and as a hysteric, imposing her own hallucinations on to the innocent children, finally at the cost of the life of one them. Felman suggests that the various frames of the narrative put the governess, the other hearers of the tale within the story, and ourselves as readers, in the position of the detective who wishes to see all and know all, to understand all that is happening in the tale: to, in Lacanian terms, have the phallus. The story's ambiguity represents the ways in which this fantasised position of mastery is unattainable. For Felman, literature itself – as a fictional form which refuses to promise a 'truth' outside itself, and which bases its discourse on the slide of meaning inherent to the signifying system of language – deconstructs the possibility of mastery (Felman 1977b; Vice 1996: 75–114).

The feminist interpretation of Lacan's ideas has also been taken up by psychoanalytic film theory, which focuses on the idea of the gaze. Watching a film is very different from reading a novel; the visual medium of film can, on the one hand, install us in the position of characters on the screen; deceptively, the camera seems to allow us literally to share their viewpoint. On the other hand, watching a film also usually means watching from a voyeuristic position of omniscience – a position which combines the (apparent) possibility of seeing, and therefore knowing, with the erotic pleasure of watching the appealing 'silver screen'. The filmic gaze can therefore, in Lacanian terminology, be equated with the fantasy of having the phallus – of watching and overseeing all from a position of power. In turn, this phallic position has been equated with a masculine one. Critics such as Laura Mulvey have suggested that the various subject positions open to the viewer who identifies with the camera, audience or characters in a film are almost inevitably structured as male. Whether we are biologically men or women, in a darkened movie theatre we all watch, for instance, Marilyn Monroe through the eyes of the masculine, desiring viewer. More than this, the very concept of narrative pleasure, a story that satisfies certain types of wishes for closure, having a beginning, middle and end, has been viewed by Mulvey and critics following her as supporting a phallic masculine fantasy of, once again, getting the 'whole story': supplementing what is missing in the Lacanian lacking subject with the fantasy of the 'whole' filmic image. Mulvey herself has since modified her initial position on the male gaze, suggesting that the dynamics of looking and identification are potentially more fluid than that original story allows (Mulvey 1989; Penley 1988).With the recent interest in cultural studies and the history of film, film theory has broadened its approach to take in new critical perspectives, but the psychoanalytic reading of film remains richly thought-provoking in work such as that of Mary Anne Doane on the *film noir* (Doane 1991).

More recently feminist and queer literary and cultural critics have taken the ideas of Freud and Lacan in new directions. One of the most important of these critics has been Judith Butler (1956–). In her influential book *Gender Trouble*, Butler argues that sex and gender, rather than being biological or natural givens, are categories that are constructed performatively through the repetition of bodily acts over time. These ideas build upon and take issue with psychoanalytic thought in a number of ways. Butler picks up on an article by the early psychoanalyst Joan Riviere (1883–1962), 'Womanliness as Masquerade', which asserts that there is no difference between 'genuine womanliness and the masquerade' (Riviere 1986). Butler goes on to suggest that sex and gender identities are structured like masquerades; our identities are not given but acted out by us everyday. However, this is not to argue that we can put on and take off our gender or sexual identity the way we put on and take off our clothes. Butler's idea of performativity refers to a performance which, in a sense, creates the subject (rather than a performance that is accomplished by a pre-existing subject). We come into being in the process of performing our sex and gender identities. (See Butler 1990 and Sarah Salih 2002, especially chapter 2, for a fuller exposition of Butler.)

We might see how this schema resembles Lacan's ideas about taking on identities within language. Rather than simply being users of language, we are always also used by language; in other words, we only ever establish our identities within and through language; it structures the ways in which we think of ourselves and everything else. And, as we know, in Lacan's reading of Freud, language is based on the loss of an original sense of (fantasised) oneness with the world connected with infancy. Butler's ideas are not identical to Lacan's or Freud's by any means. But she does pick up on this idea of loss. Using Freud's ideas about loss from 'Mourning and Melancholia', Butler goes on to argue that the formation of sex and gender identity may also be a question of loss. If, as Freud suggests, as infants we find ourselves both identifying with and desiring both sexes in the form of our parents, then at some point, in order to comply with the Oedipal law (or culture's requirements, depending upon your perspective), we must all give up on one set of these identifications and desires. As a girl, in order to become heterosexual, you must relinquish loving your mother and identifying with your father so that you can direct your desire towards men and your identification toward women. (If you are homosexual it is the other way round.) Freud's ideas about melancholia suggested that the melancholic identifies with the lost object in such a way as to be almost haunted by that object (see pp. 87–89). *Gender Trouble*, in a sense, suggests that we are all haunted by our repudiated identifications and desires. Performing one version of identity (and having it perform us) also means living with the after-effects of the sexual choices we relinquished – heterosexuality or homosexuality. Our performances are, in a sense, premised on what we have lost. (See Salih 2002: 52–8 for a much fuller explication of this argument.)

Critics of gender and sexuality such as Butler and Eve Kosofsky Sedgwick (1950–) read Freud closely to analyse his own blind spots (such as his tendency to fall back on the assumption that the masculine or the heterosexual is the norm, from which all other tendencies deviate), but also to tease out the hidden assumptions and implications of psychoanalytic ideas. In her book *Between Men* Eve Sedgwick suggests, like Freud in the Oedipus complex, that desire may be triangulated, played out between three people rather than two. In many nineteenth-century novels we find a scenario which involves two men apparently fighting over the love of a woman. Sedgwick argues that if we pay close attention to the language of these works we often find that the erotic tension is played out more forcefully between the two men. The men are really more interested in each other than either of them is in the woman (even if that interest may look at times violent or hate-filled). (See Sedgwick 1985; Edwards 2008.) Feminist critics and queer theorists have creatively used Freudian logic to show the many ways in which desire, sexuality and the realm of unconscious life may help us analyse both our literature and our lives.

Freud's reading techniques, as refined and refracted through Lacan's insistence upon the interrelatedness of language, sexed identity and desire, has come to rest in many different areas of critical theory. Even when Freud himself is seen as participating in a historically confined sexism in his psychic placement of women as men without penises, his ideas about the constructed nature of gender identity and the multiple identifications with, and desires for, the multiple positions of the Oedipal situation have created waves in many areas of modern literary and cultural criticism. In academia, many of us will continue to look at the world through Freud-coloured glasses, arguing virulently against his more exasperating positions, when we are not employing, and acting out, his theories of reading.

BACKLASH AND CONTINUED RELEVANCE

Freud had one sure-fire way of disarming his critics; turning his own weapons against them, he claimed that any denial of psychoanalytic findings was based on resistance to the upsetting and sexual nature of his discoveries. In this final section, tempting as it may be, I will try not to follow Freud's lead by diagnosing those who vilify him as neurotic or repressed. Rather I will follow through one particular strand of criticism of Freud, hoping to understand the emotional impetus behind it, as well as to uncover some of its potentially flawed assumptions.

The backlash against Freud has been felt less in the discipline of literary criticism than in other arenas of public debate, although it has also affected literary studies. A turn in literary criticism towards cultural studies and an emphasis on the specificity of historical factors in understanding works of literature have made Freudian readings of the crudely universalising type – which see a phallus in every extended object, whatever its context or historical moment – much less popular. Rather, more sophisticated psychoanalytic literary studies have come to accept that reading literature through Freud's ideas is not enough: one must simultaneously read Freud as literature and contextualise Freud in history.

Over the past years, in other disciplines and in the press, there has been a veritable onslaught of Freud-bashing from scientists, therapists, doctors and historians, to name but a few. As I have presented Freud, he is a theoretician whose ideas are often speculative and undoubtedly contentious. But contentious, influential thinkers – philosophers, for instance – rarely provoke the kind of ire that Freud does. Even Karl Marx, a thinker whose political influence has been widely felt and recently, and violently, rejected by many, rarely seems to raise the spectre of personal hatred that Freud does. What is it that Freud's thought suggests, or questions, that makes him appear so dangerous to such a wide variety of critics? And what, finally, can we take away from psychoanalysis?

Alongside the feminist critique of psychoanalysis I discussed in the last section, there have been a number of critiques of Freud's claims to the status of psychoanalysis as a science, often based on the lack of data that can be adduced about psychoanalytic cures. A more personal critique of Freud accuses him variously of being addicted to cocaine, lying about his patients, having an affair with his sister-in-law, or all of the above. Finally there is the contention that psychoanalysis simply does not work – analytic therapy does not cure people as well as anti-depressant drugs do. These attacks cannot be fully dealt with in the space of this conclusion. I urge readers to go to the 'Further reading' section and discover for themselves the case against Freud, to balance the case I am making here for him. Here I will focus on one of the most influential of the attacks on Freud – the attack on his theory of fantasy.

One source of the 'Freud Wars', as they have been labelled, can be found in Freud's early attempts to elaborate the origins of sexual desire in children. The emphasis of psychoanalysis on fantasy as potentially formative of the individual mind has raised many outraged and dissenting voices. Critics have accused psychoanalysis of denying the effects of history or the 'real event', which impinges upon a person from the outside, in favour of psychical reality – the inner desires, fantasies and repressions which can become equivalent to reality for the subject. Jeffrey Masson's 1984 book *The Assault on Truth: Freud's Suppression of the Seduction Theory* set off the first wave of this attack on Freud in recent times. Masson claims that Freud's initial postulation of the seduction theory was correct: Freud's patients were, in fact, sexually assaulted by their fathers (see Chapter 1). According to Masson, when Freud renounced the seduction theory in favour of the theory of fantasy, he betrayed his women patients, to whom he had promised to listen. In the 1970s feminists critical of Freud used this critique as an example of Freud's insensitivity to his women patients. The talking cure was based, importantly, on someone listening – but was it necessarily based on that listener also believing that what he or she heard was true? According to Masson it was. By moving from belief in the real world of events to a focus on the staged, and therefore inauthentic, world of psychic fantasy, Freud denied the reality of his patients' pain and abuse and destroyed their trust.

Psychoanalysis responds to this charge by emphasising that a focus on psychical reality – the ways in which fantasy takes on the force of reality for the patient – does not by any means imply that traumatising events don't happen to people in the 'real' world. Events, and sometimes horrible ones, do happen all the time. But the psychic world of the individual must somehow then process – or, in the case of trauma, refuse to process – these events. Things that occur in the outside world are always interpreted, understood, re-staged by the mind. The psyche stages itself for a variety of unconscious motivations, but that in no way makes its dramas inauthentic to the person who experiences them.

Debates in the press about what is alternatively called recovered memory or false memory syndrome have also returned to Freud to criticise his theories of fantasy and/or repression. Both sides of these debates – those who believe in the prevalence of childhood sexual abuse and the repression of memories, and those who believe in the possibility of false memory syndrome or the implantation of false memories into minds of patients by the suggestions of therapists – employ and condemn psychoanalysis strategically to support their cases. For believers in repressed memory, Freud tragically betrayed his hysterical women patients when he disavowed their stories of sexual abuse, instead founding psychoanalysis on the idea that fantasy could have psychic effects which were as deep-rooted and far-reaching as reality. But if, for the supporters of repressed memory theory, Freud was the first in a long line of villains to disbelieve the horrifying stories he heard, he also forged the theory of psychic trauma, in which an event (such as a sexual assault) that takes place in childhood could remain unconscious and unremembered until triggered into experience by another event later in life. The traumatic Freud understood the possibility of repressed memory, even if the post-seduction-theory Freud denied the reality of childhood sexual abuse. For those who support the existence of false memory syndrome – and point to a boom industry in suggestive therapists milking suggestible patients through twelve-step treatments to uncover alien encounters and satanic rituals (as well as childhood abuse) – the two Freuds are reversed. The Freud who recognised that fantasy could be as formative as reality is given some grudging credit, while the Freud whose deceptive unconscious opened up the possibility of repressed memory is taken to task. Either way Freud loses.

But what all these debates show is that the theories of psychoanalysis do more work – are more convincing and suggestive – when we see them as exploring the ways in which fantasy or fiction contributes to our own construction and understanding of our identities, rather than trying to use Freud's theories to judge events according to the standards of evidential truth or falsity. This is not to say that events should not be judged according to these standards. There are many arenas of life in which those standards are vitally necessary – a courtroom, for instance. But perhaps psychoanalysis is not at its most useful in those arenas. Freud's concept of fantasy is based in the world of psychic reactions we all have, all the time: reactions to things that happen to us, but also to things that don't happen to us – things that we wish for, fear or imagine happening. The focus of psychoanalysis on fantasy brackets off the question of whether events really happened or not, taking an attitude to history similar to the one that literature might be seen to take. When we read a novel the question of its truth or accuracy does not necessarily enter into our experience of it; rather our reactions tend to be about how the novel affects us, whether it seems emotionally true (rather than objectively true), whether it makes us think about things in new ways or whether it fictionally fulfils our wishes or desires. Of course two people meeting for therapy in a psychoanalytic office is not a situation equivalent to someone sitting down to read a novel; what is at stake is very different. But yet, as I suggested earlier, the forms of transference involved may be similar; the question of constructing a past that will help to explain the present and forge a future can be seen as a question of reading and interpretation, and, as our continuing cultural fascination with psychoanalysis shows, Freud continues to provide challenging and provocative ways for thinking-through this question.

John Forrester (1997: 5) has suggested that the attempt to ascertain the status of psychoanalysis as art or science is a mistaken approach to the continuing cultural irritation that is Freud: 'We have to take seriously the suggestion that debates about psychoanalysis should not be couched in the form: is it an art or a science? But rather: what changes in our general categories are required by recognizing that psychoanalysis is both an art *and* a science?' Forrester continues: 'psychoanalysis has produced in the analyst a cultural figure whose work is aesthetic as much as it is investigative (in the style of the research scientist or of the private detective) and has made available to the patient the opportunity to render his or her life a work of art, a narrative of chance and destiny as well as a thriller, whether psychological or otherwise' (Forrester 1997: 5). Psychoanalytic criticism, at its best, raises as many questions as it answers about the difference between art and science, fact and fiction, fantasy and reality; about the status of authority figures; about the ways we come to think we know what we desire or think we know who we are; about the knowledge we claim to hold about ourselves and others. As far as I can see, none of Freud's attackers has begun to provide methods for approaching questions of this depth to take the place of the interpretive schema they are so eager to discard. I predict that, in academia and out of it, Freud's works will continue to be read, and continue to help people to read differently, even as they continue to provoke both fractious dissension and eager agreement, long into the twenty-first century.

FURTHER READING

BIBLIOGRAPHICAL NOTE

Quotations from Freud have been taken from the following two editions of his work:

SE: *Standard Edition of the Complete Psychological Works of Sigmund Freud* (1953–74), trans. James Strachey, London: Hogarth Press and Institute of Psychoanalysis. The standard work in English.

PFL: *Penguin Freud Library* (1991–93), ed. Angela Richards and Albert Dickson, London: Penguin. Less complete, but more easily available. When a work not included in the Penguin Freud Library is referred to in the text, the page reference is to the Standard Edition.

Penguin have begun an entirely new translation of Freud's works with Adam Phillips as general editor. For simplicity's sake I have confined myself to the earlier Penguin Freud Library edition, which reproduces the Strachey translations of the Standard Edition. Freud's output was enormous. Writing an introduction to his work necessitates taking material from many different sources. Because so many of Freud's texts are referred to in detail and in passing in the body of this volume, what follows is a selected list of some of his most important and most accessible works. The 'Works cited' section at the end of the volume includes the complete list of works that appear in this volume.

WORKS BY SIGMUND FREUD

Freud, S. and Breuer J. *Studies on Hysteria* (1895), SE 2; PFL 3. These fascinating case studies are an excellent starting point for understanding the origins of psychoanalysis. See particularly Breuer's case of Anna O., who coined the phrase 'talking cure', and Freud's cases of Emmy von N. and Elizabeth von R.

Freud, S. *The Interpretation of Dreams* (1900), SE 4–5; PFL 4. His *Dream* book was the work that Freud himself saw as his most significant. It is long – read it selectively if you are in a hurry – but there's no better place to look for the psychoanalytic reading technique laid out.

——*The Psychopathology of Everyday Life* (1901), SE 6; PFL 5. Freud's exploration of the workings of unconscious desires in our everyday experience, through slips of the tongue, forgotten words and mistaken actions, makes entertaining reading. Like *Jokes and their Relation to the Unconscious* (which, despite its title, is not at all funny), *The Psychopathology of Everyday Life* primarily consists of a few excellent theoretical points hidden amongst an extended list of examples.

——'Fragment of an Analysis of a Case of Hysteria (Dora)' (1905), SE 7: 1–122; PFL 8: 29–164. This is the classic case study that shows Freud at his least able to answer the question 'What does woman want?' It has been a taking-off point for many important feminist analyses – see Bernheimer and Kahane (1985).

——*Three Essays on the Theory of Sexuality* (1905), SE 7: 123–245; PFL 7: 32–169. Along with *The Interpretation of Dreams* this is probably Freud's most important and ground-breaking work. He revised it continuously over his lifetime. It is the main place to go for his theories of the stages of sexual development and the perversions.

——'Civilized Sexual Morality and Modern Nervous Illness' (1908), SE 9: 177–204; PFL 12: 27–55. This is Freud's earliest discussion of the conflict between civilisation and instinctual life which becomes central to his theories in works such as *Civilization and its Discontents*.

——'Notes upon a Case of Obsessional Neurosis (the Rat Man)' (1909), SE 10: 155–249; PFL 9: 33–128. Of Freud's major case histories, this is undoubtedly his most successful. His readings of the Rat Man's obsessive ideas are stark and original.

———*Five Lectures on Psychoanalysis* (1910), SE 11: 13–55. These were given as a series of lectures by Freud in America in 1909. This slim collection is still the best very short introduction to Freud's major ideas that you can find.

———'Leonardo da Vinci and a Memory of his Childhood' (1910), SE 11: 57–137; PFL 14: 145–231. Freud analyses one of Leonardo's paintings and discovers homosexuality and a mother complex. It probably won't convince you that psychoanalytic interpretations of art are worth the paper they're printed on, but there are some interesting ideas about mother love hidden in here.

———'Psychoanalytic Notes on an Autobiographical Account of a Case of Paranoia (Schreber)' (1911), SE 12: 1–82; PFL 9: 131–223. Freud analyses the writings of a psychotic judge who was hospitalised for many years before publishing his story. It is a fascinating piece, and there has been some good recent criticism about it. This is the place to go for Freud's controversial theorising of the linkage between paranoia and homosexuality.

———*Totem and Taboo* (1912–13), SE 13: 1–162; PFL 13: 49–235. Freud's most speculative foray into the field of anthropology; this piece reads like a fairy story, but a fascinating one.

———'On Narcissism' (1914), SE 14: 67–102; PFL 11: 59–97. 'On Narcissism' is an important but difficult article in which Freud wrestles with the definitions of many concepts that become central to psychoanalysis in the 1920s and 1930s. It discusses the importance of infantile narcissism to development and introduces the idea of the ego ideal that later becomes the basis for the super-ego.

———'Remembering, Repeating and Working Through' (1914), SE 12: 147–56. The 'working through' of resistances is a fundamental part of the analytic process. This short article does not finally define the term in a completely satisfying way, but it is worth reading none the less.

———'On the History of the Psychoanalytic Movement' (1914), SE 14: 7–66; PFL 15: 59–127. Watch out for this one – Freud wrote it at a moment when he was particularly bitter towards some of his ex-friends (such as Jung) and beleaguered by criticisms and attacks. It is a very defensive text, interesting in lots of ways, but by no means perfect as an introduction.

——'Mourning and Melancholia' (1917), SE 14: 237–58; PFL 11: 245–68. This short article is one of Freud's most compelling. He returns again to the problem of loss; psychoanalysis is replete with images of loss, but he is rarely this eloquent.

——'From the History of an Infantile Neurosis (the Wolf Man)' (1918), SE 17: 1–122; PFL 9: 227–366. In this case history Freud defines extremely important psychoanalytic concepts such as construction and the primal scene.

——'The "Uncanny"' (1919), SE 17: 217–52; PFL 14: 339–76. A fascinating mixture of Freud's ideas about the origins of a particular kind of fear – combines literary criticism and his speculations on anthropology.

——'The Psychogenesis of a Case of Homosexuality in a Woman' (1920), SE 18: 145–72; PFL 9: 367–400. This short case history, along with the Schreber case, is a good place to look for the strengths and weaknesses of Freud's theorising of homosexuality.

——*Beyond the Pleasure Principle* (1920), SE 18: 7–64; PFL 11: 269–338. This is one of Freud's oddest and most compulsive works. It contains his ideas about the repetition compulsion and the death drive. It has been a key text for further post-structuralist readings of Freud (see, particularly, Derrida 1987).

——'Group Psychology and the Analysis of the Ego' (1921), SE 18: 65–143; PFL 12: 91–178. In this fascinating article Freud explores questions about the relationship between crowd behaviour and individual psychology. It's good to read this along with *Totem and Taboo* and *Civilization and its Discontents*.

——'The Ego and the Id' (1923), SE 19: 1–66; PFL 11: 339–406. This one sounds like it's just what you want to explain Freud's basic concepts, but it is in fact very dense and difficult. In it Freud theorises his concept of the bodily ego.

——'An Autobiographical Study' (1925), SE 20: 3–74; PFL 15: 185–260. Although this contains some interesting autobiographical touches, it is much more the story of psychoanalysis the institution than of Freud the person. It gives a more balanced perspective than 'On the History of the Psychoanalytic Movement'. If you want Freud's life story see Jones (1953–57) or Gay (1989).

————'Some Psychical Consequences of the Anatomical Distinction between the Sexes' (1925), SE 19: 241–58; PFL 7: 323–43. This is a good short piece to compare with *Three Essays on Sexuality*, to see the ways in which Freud becomes more entrenched in his ideas of feminine sexuality and penis envy in his old age.

————'Civilization and its Discontents' (1930), SE 21: 57–145; PFL 12: 243–340. The best single piece you can read for Freud's take on modern society; Freud at his crabbiest but full of delights.

WORKS ON SIGMUND FREUD

Appignanesi, L. and Forrester, J. *Freud's Women* (1992), London: Virago. This dauntingly large volume is good for background on Freud's women patients, colleagues and relations.

Appignanesi, R. and Zarate, O. *Introducing Freud* (1999), Cambridge: Icon Books. This comic-book version of Freud's ideas is an entertaining and painless way to get the basics with illustrations.

Bernheimer, C. and Kahane, C. (eds) *In Dora's Case: Freud–Hysteria–Feminism* (1985), London: Virago. This collection is a psychoanalytic feminist classic. It contains extremely helpful articles on 'Dora' by many important psychoanalytic critics, including Jacqueline Rose, Neil Hertz and Jane Gallop.

Crews, F. *et al. The Memory Wars: Freud's Legacy in Dispute* (1995), New York: New York Review of Books. Crews was a rabidly enthusiastic psychoanalytic critic who later renounced psychoanalysis with great vigour. This collection includes hypercritical articles about Freud he wrote for the *New York Review of Books* and a selection of the letters they published in response.

Falkland, G. *Freud's Literary Culture* (2000), Cambridge: Cambridge University Press. An analysis of the ways in which Freud's reading of Goethe, Sophocles, Shakespeare and others influenced the formation of psychoanalysis.

Forrester, J. *Dispatches from the Freud Wars: Psychoanalysis and its Passions* (1997), Cambridge MA: Harvard University Press. Forrester's book is one of the best places to turn to for cogent analyses of the backlash against Freud from a psychoanalytic sympathiser.

Gay, P. *Freud: A Life for our Time* (1989), London: Macmillan. This is a compulsively readable biography of Freud. However, if you're looking for critical distance go elsewhere. Gay is almost as admiring of Freud as Freud's devoted follower Ernest Jones, who wrote the first worshipful biography of the Great Man (see next entry).

Jones, E. *Sigmund Freud: Life and Work* (1953–57), Vols I–III, London: Hogarth Press. Jones's uncritical attitude to Freud can be exasperating at times but this is still a fascinating biography of a fascinating mind, written by someone who was on the scene at the time.

Laplanche, J. and Pontalis, J.-B. *The Language of Psychoanalysis* (1973), trans. D. Nicholson-Smith, New York: Norton. This is by far the best dictionary of psychoanalytic terms available, but it is also much more than that. Although published in the early 1970s it still contains the smartest and most accurate explanations of Freud's terminology. Advanced, though.

Lesser, R.C. and Schoenberg, E. (eds) *That Obscure Object of Desire: Freud's Female Homosexual Revisited* (1999), New York: Routledge. Contains Freud's 'A Case of Female Homosexuality' and a series of articles about it from academics and practising analysts.

Mahony, P.J. *Freud as a Writer* (1987), New Haven CT: Yale University Press. A readable, straightforward exploration of the power of Freud's rhetoric.

Marcus, Laura (ed.) *Sigmund Freud's* The Interpretation of Dreams: *New Interdisciplinary Essays* (1999), Manchester: Manchester University Press. This is a good collection of essays on *The Interpretation of Dreams* to mark its hundredth birthday.

Masson, J. *The Assault on Truth: Freud's Suppression of the Seduction Theory* (1984), New York: Farrar Straus & Giroux. Masson's scathing attack on Freud's ethics and the origin of psychoanalysis got lots of press attention when it was published. Masson claims that Freud turned his back on the real abuse suffered by his early hysterical women patients when he began to doubt their stories of early childhood seduction. For Masson, psychoanalysis is founded on this suppression of Freud's, and Freud is undoubtedly the villain of the piece. Although Masson's book was popularly influential, it is extremely reductive and limited in its understanding of Freudian concepts. Read it critically if you read it at all.

Neu, J. (ed.) *The Cambridge Companion to Freud* (1991), Cambridge: Cambridge University Press. A collection that leans towards the philosophical questions that Freud's work provokes.

Rieff, P. *Freud: The Mind of the Moralist* (1959), Chicago: University of Chicago Press. Rieff's work is invaluable as a wonderful, early thinking-through of the moral and ethical questions that analysis raises.

Storr, A. *Freud* (1989), Oxford: Oxford University Press. A short, engagingly written, but very selective, lay-person's guide to Freud.

Surprenant, C. *Freud: A Guide for the Perplexed* (2008), London: Continuum. A rigorous philosophical guide that respects the complexity of Freud's key ideas and is especially good on Freud's topography and economic theories.

Wollheim, R. *Freud* (1971), London: Fontana. Unbeatable for accuracy and sophistication, this advanced guide to Freud's ideas and stages of his thought is probably not for beginners.

FURTHER READING IN PSYCHOANALYTIC CRITICISM

Bloom, H. *The Anxiety of Influence: A Theory of Poetry* (1973), New York: Oxford University Press. Bloom applies Freud's Oedipal theory to poets, arguing that strong poets must metaphorically kill off their poetic forefathers in order to carve a place for themselves in the canon of tradition. Very influential when it was first written, it has since been criticised from several angles, including feminist theory.

Bowie, M. *Lacan* (1991), London: Harvard University Press. This is probably the most accurate and well written explication of Lacan available.

Bowlby, R. *Freudian Mythologies: Greek Tragedy and Modern Identities* (2007), Oxford: Oxford University Press. Engaging exploration of the ways in which the shifting face of the modern family and modern sexual relations may affect the way we understand the many psychoanalytic ideas that Freud takes from his readings of Greek mythology.

Brennan, T. (ed.) *Between Feminism and Psychoanalysis* (1989), London and New York: Routledge. This is a somewhat dated, but still cogent, collection of articles exploring the ways in which French feminist theory has used and critiqued psychoanalysis.

Brooks, P. *Reading for the Plot: Design and Intention in Narrative* (1985), New York: Vintage. Brooks's book contains excellent analyses of a number of English and European novels.

Burgin, V., Donald, J. and Kaplan C. (eds) *Formations of Fantasy* (1986), London: Routledge. Contains extremely important articles by Riviere, Heath and Laplanche and Pontalis which explore the complex issues surrounding Freud's notion of fantasy.

Butler, J. *Gender Trouble: Feminism and the Subversion of Identity* (1990), New York: Routledge. Butler's sophisticated and rigorous philosophical readings of the performative nature of gender and sexuality have been incredibly influential. More recent work, such as *The Psychic Life of Power* (see next two books), reads psychoanalysis alongside the work of Michel Foucault to explore melancholia and psychic dynamics in relation to power and the political.

——*Bodies that Matter: On the Discursive Limits of 'Sex'* (1993), New York: Routledge.

——*The Psychic Life of Power: Theories in Subjection* (1997), Stanford CA: Stanford University Press.

Derrida, J. 'Freud and the Scene of Writing', in *Writing and Difference* (1978), trans. Alan Bass, London: Routledge, 196–230. Derrida responds to Freud's short article 'The Mystic Writing Pad'. This is a very difficult piece but key for establishing the deconstructive reading of Freud.

——*The Postcard: From Socrates to Freud and Beyond* (1987), trans. Alan Bass, Chicago: University of Chicago Press. Continuing in Derrida's difficult style, it contains important articles about Lacan and *Beyond the Pleasure Principle*.

Doane, M. *Femmes fatales: Feminism, Film Theory, Psychoanalysis* (1991), London: Routledge. Doane's work on film theory is sharp and provocative. A good place to look for skilful psychoanalytic readings of individual films.

Ellmann, M. (ed.) *Psychoanalytic Literary Criticism* (1994), London: Longman. This is still the best recent collection of articles on psychoanalysis and literature. Ellman's introduction is invaluable, and Cynthia Chase's article 'Oedipal Textuality: Reading Freud's Reading of *Oedipus*' is a classic reading of Sophocles with Freud.

Fanon, F. *Black Skin, White Masks* (1986), London: Pluto. Originally published in 1952, Fanon's semi-autobiographical exploration of racism analyses its roots as deeply embedded in the psychic patterns of the West. His work becomes a taking-off point for analyses of colonialism and postcolonialism which engage with psychoanalytic thinking.

Felman, S. 'Turning the Screw of Interpretation', *Yale French Studies* (1977), 55/56: 94–207. Felman's *tour de force* Lacanian reading of Henry James's uncanny tale 'The Turn of the Screw' brilliantly describes the relationship between literature and transference. It has dated, however, in that its reliance on a certain kind of deconstructive rhetoric that flourished in the 1970s now appears somewhat overblown and decontextualised. The close readings are none the less masterly.

Foucault, M. *The History of Sexuality*, Vol. I (1990), trans. R. Hurley, London: Penguin. One of the founding texts of queer theory. Foucault argues that sex and modern sexuality are a discursive formation, and that the nineteenth century, which we tend to see as the historical moment when discussion of sex was repressed, really coincides with an explosion of sexual discourses. Foucault sees Freudian psychoanalysis as one in a series of modern medical and juridical discourses of power which produces sex as the secret truth of the self.

Gallop. J. *The Daughter's Seduction: Feminism and Psychoanalysis* (1982), Ithaca NY: Cornell University Press. An early sharp feminist critique of Freud. Gallop's provocative style is always fun to read, if often contentious. One of her specialities is deflating the phallus.

Grosz, E. *Jacques Lacan: A Feminist Introduction* (1990), London: Routledge. Useful as an overview of the often vexed relationship between feminism and Lacanian psychoanalysis.

Gunn, D. *Psychoanalysis and Fiction* (1988), Cambridge: Cambridge University Press. Penetrating readings of the writings of psychoanalytic practitioners and analysts as well as Kafka, Beckett, Proust and more through a broadly Lacanian framework. Highly intelligent.

Klein, M. *The Selected Melanie Klein* (1985), ed. Juliet Mitchell, London: Penguin Books. An excellent collection which contains many of Klein's more accessible works. The introduction by Juliet Mitchell is also very helpful.

Kristeva, J. *Desire in Language: A Semiotic Approach to Literature and Art* (1980), trans T. Gorz, A. Jardine and L. Roudiez, Oxford: Blackwell.

——*Powers of Horror: An Essay on Abjection* (1982), trans. L. Roudiez, New York: Columbia University Press.

——*Black Sun: Depression and Melancholia* (1989), trans. L. Roudiez, New York: Columbia University Press. Kristeva's combination of psychoanalysis and French feminist critiques of language is still challenging to read, and her analyses of specific works of literature are often compelling. Her more recent work flounders in some dodgy political waters, but her early books, especially *Powers of Horror* and *Black Sun*, create a fascinating poetics of the feminine. Definitely not for beginners. Go to Moi (1985) first if it's all too frightening.

Lane, C. (ed.) *The Psychoanalysis of Race* (1998), New York: Columbia University Press. This collection contains a good introduction by Lane and many interesting essays exploring the intersection of race and psychoanalysis in subjects from Julia Kristeva to W.E.B. Dubois. It also boasts Slavoj Žižek's wonderfully entitled 'Love thy Neighbor? No, thanks!'

Lebeau, V. *Psychoanalysis and Cinema: The Play of Shadows* (2001), London: Wallflower Press. A short but compelling exploration of the intertwined historical development of cinema and psychoanalysis, through their shared interest in dreams, desires, images and shocks, amongst other topics.

Meltzer, F. (ed.) *The Trial(s) of Psychoanalysis* (1988), Chicago: University of Chicago Press. This excellent collection contains Stanley Fish's entertaining and brutal, yet thought-provoking, attack on Freud's rhetoric, 'Withholding the Missing Portion', Peter Brooks's useful article 'The Idea of a Psychoanalytic Literary Criticism' and Arnold I. Davidson's fantastic Foucauldian reading of Freud's *Three Essays on the Theory of Sexuality*.

Mitchell, J. *Psychoanalysis and Feminism* (1974), New York: Pantheon. Mitchell's important book began the reclaiming of psychoanalysis for feminism in England.

Mitchell, J. and Rose, J., introductions to J. Lacan *Feminine Sexuality: Jacques Lacan and the École freudienne* (1985), New York: Norton. Mitchell's and Rose's separate introductions to this collection of writings of Lacan on women are invaluable for charting the relationship between Freud's and Lacan's ideas about sexuality.

Moi, T. *Sexual/Textual Politics: Feminist Literary Theory* (1985), London: Methuen. Although now somewhat dated in terms of recent developments in feminism, this book is still the best starting point for understanding the arguments between Anglo-American and French feminism, and how psychoanalysis fits into those debates.

Mulvey, L. *Visual and other Pleasures* (1989), Basingstoke: Macmillan. Mulvey's influential 1975 article 'Visual Pleasure and Narrative Cinema', included in this collection, began a new discussion about the 'gaze' and sexual difference in film theory.

Phillips, A. *On Kissing, Tickling and being Bored* (1993), Cambridge MA: Harvard University Press. Phillips's short articles on psychoanalysis (in this and the next two books) are compulsively readable and extremely entertaining. A practising analyst himself, his work is committed to making complicated analytic ideas accessible and connected with real life.

——*On Flirtation* (1994), London: Faber.

——*Promises, Promises* (2000), London: Faber.

Rose. J. *Sexuality in the Field of Vision* (1986), London: Verso. This collection of Rose's articles contains difficult but excellent explanations of the importance of Lacan to feminism and to theories of the visual, as well as interesting feminist psychoanalytic readings of George Eliot and *Hamlet*.

——*The Haunting of Sylvia Plath* (1991), London: Virago. A brilliant example of how psychoanalytic reading can yield rich literary results in the case of a single author.

——*Why War? Psychoanalysis, Politics and the Return to Melanie Klein* (1993), Oxford: Blackwell. Rose's work (in this and the next two books) continues to explore the intersections of psychoanalysis, politics and culture. Much of her recent work has been devoted to Zionism and the Israel–Palestine conflict.

——*On Not Being Able to Sleep: Psychoanalysis and the Modern World* (2003), London: Chatto & Windus.

——*The Last Resistance* (2007), London: Verso.

Royle, N. *The Uncanny* (2003), Manchester: Manchester University Press. A fantastic spinning out of Freud's marvellous essay on the uncanny in all sorts of fun and provocative directions from Shakespeare to Dickens to Dostoevsky to Derrida. A big book but easy to dip into.

Sedgwick, E.K. *Between Men: English Literature and Male Homosocial Desire* (1985), New York: Columbia University Press.

——*The Epistemology of the Closet* (1990), London: Penguin. In this and the preceding book Sedgwick uses and critiques psychoanalysis's analyses of homosexuality to argue for the central importance of the homo/hetero binary to understanding Western culture. If you are intrigued by the idea of queer theory the chapter in *Epistemology of the Closet* entitled 'Axiomatic' will take your breath away.

Showalter, E. *The Female Malady: Women, Madness, and English Culture, 1830–1980* (1985), New York: Penguin. Showalter's work on nineteenth-century women and madness seems a bit dated now, but it is still a useful starting point for thinking about the cultural context from which Freud's ideas about women emerge.

Vice, S. (ed.) *Psychoanalytic Criticism: A Reader* (1996), Cambridge: Polity Press. This is a useful collection which juxtaposes psychoanalytic articles of general interest with specific psychoanalytic readings of texts such as Virginia Woolf's *Mrs Dalloway* and Toni Morrison's *Beloved*. It contains extracts from several classic essays, including Shoshona Felman's article on Henry James, 'Turning the Screw of Interpretation', and Peter Brooks's 'Freud's Masterplot'. Be aware of the limitations of extracted essays, however.

Warner, M. 'Homo-narcissism: or, Heterosexuality' in J. Boone and M. Cadden (eds), *Engendering Men: The Question of Male Feminist Criticism* (1990), London: Routledge. Warner's article criticises Freud's linking of narcissism with homosexuality and shows the ways in which this perception of homosexuality underpins modern notions of heterosexuality.

Wright, E. *Psychoanalytic Criticism: Theory in Practice* (1984), London: Methuen. Wright's book is densely written, but helpful for tracing the history of psychoanalytic criticism after Freud but before the current climate.

Žižek, S. *The Sublime Object of Ideology* (1989), London: Verso. The versatile and entertaining cultural and political critic Žižek has written many books which highlight his particular blend of Marx, Lacan and popular culture but this early one is one of his best. He jumps from Jewish jokes to Kant to Hitchcock to Tom and Jerry in an arresting display of the ways in which psychoanalysis can contribute to political and philosophical analyses of the contemporary world.

INTERNET RESOURCES

Because of copyright issues, very few of Freud's writings are available in full on line, but here are some other useful sources.

www.freud.org.uk, the website of the Freud Museum in London. The Freud Museum is located in the house Freud lived in for the final years of his life, 20 Maresfield Gardens, Hampstead. The house remained the home of Freud's youngest daughter, Anna, an important analyst in her own right, until her death in 1982. The museum's website provides information for researchers, photographs of Freud and his family, links to other Freud sources and information about conferences and exhibits.

http://psychclassics.yorku.ca, Classics in the history of psychology. This website makes available electronically the full text of a number of scholarly works on the history of psychology. It contains early, pre-Standard Edition translations of *The Psychopathology of Everyday Life* and *The Interpretation of Dreams*, among other works.

http://webspace.ship.edu/cgboer/freud.html. This page provides a biography of Freud and an outline of his theories from early conceptions to later drafts.

www.cyberpsych.org/apf/, American Psychoanalytic Foundation. A reading list of articles and books on psychoanalysis.

www.freud-museum.at/e/, website of the Freud Museum, Vienna.

www.freudfile.org/ provides information about the life and work of Sigmund Freud.

www.loc.gov/exhibits/freud/, the site of the Library of Congress 'Conflict and Culture' exhibit on Freud (2001). Interesting for the images it contains, including portraits of Freud, his family and some of his patients.

http://nyfreudian.org/abstracts_00.html, the New York Freudian Society. Abstracts of the Standard Edition of the Psychological Works of Sigmund Freud.

www.melanie-klein-trust.org.uk, a site to promote the work of Melanie Klein.

WORKS CITED

FREUD

All references in the text to Freud's work are to the Penguin Freud Library (PFL) edition unless the article is not available in that edition, in which case the page reference is to the Standard Edition (SE). (See beginning of Further Reading (p. 135) section for full details of both publications.)

Freud, S. and Breuer J. (1895) *Studies on Hysteria*, SE 2; PFL 3.

Freud, S. (1896) 'The Aetiology of Hysteria', SE 3: 189–221.

——(1900) *The Interpretation of Dreams*, SE 4–5; PFL 4.

——(1901) *The Psychopathology of Everyday Life*, SE 6; PFL 5.

——(1905a) 'Fragment of an Analysis of a Case of Hysteria (Dora)', SE 7: 1–122; PFL 8: 29–164.

——(1905b) *Three Essays on the Theory of Sexuality*, SE 7: 123–245: PFL 7: 32–169.

——(1905c) *Jokes and their Relation to the Unconscious*, SE 8; PFL 4.

——(1907a) 'Delusions and Dreams in Jensen's *Gradiva*', SE 9: 1–95; PFL 14: 27–118.

——(1907b) 'The Sexual Enlightenment of Children', SE 9: 129–39; PFL 7: 172–81.

——(1908a) 'Creative Writers and Day-dreaming', SE 9: 141–53; PFL 14: 129–41.

——(1908b) 'Civilized Sexual Morality and Modern Nervous Illness', SE 9: 177–204; PFL 12: 27–55.

——(1908c) 'Character and Anal Erotism', SE 9: 167–75: PFL 7: 205–15.

——(1909) 'Notes upon a Case of Obsessional Neurosis (the Rat Man)', SE 10: 155–249; PFL 9: 33–128.

——(1910a) *Five Lectures on Psychoanalysis*, SE 11: 13–55.

——(1910b) 'Leonardo da Vinci and a Memory of his Childhood', SE 11: 57–137; PFL 14: 145–231.

——(1911) 'Psychoanalytic Notes on an Autobiographical Account of a Case of Paranoia (Schreber)', SE 12: 1–82; PFL 9: 131–223.

——(1912–13) *Totem and Taboo*, SE 13: 1–162; PFL 13: 49–235.

——(1914a) 'The *Moses* of Michelangelo', SE 13: 209–36; PFL 14: 249–80

——(1914b) 'On Narcissism', SE 14: 67–102; PFL 11: 59–97.

——(1914c) 'Remembering, Repeating and Working Through', SE 12: 147–56.

——(1914d) 'On the History of the Psychoanalytic Movement', SE 14: 7–66; PFL 15: 59–127.

——(1915a) 'Thoughts for the Time on War and Death', SE 14: 273–300; PFL 12: 57–89.

——(1915b) 'Instincts and their Vicissitudes', SE 14: 109–40; PFL 11: 105–43.

——(1916–17) *Introductory Lectures on Psychoanalysis*, SE 15–16; PFL 1.

——(1917) 'Mourning and Melancholia', SE 14: 237–58; PFL 11: 245–68.

——(1918) 'From the History of an Infantile Neurosis (the Wolf Man)', SE 17: 1–122; PFL 9: 227–366.

——(1919) 'The "Uncanny"', SE 17: 217–52; PFL 14: 339–76.

——(1920a) 'The Psychogenesis of a Case of Homosexuality in a Woman', SE 18: 145–72; PFL 9: 367–400.

——(1920b) *Beyond the Pleasure Principle*, SE 18: 7–64; PFL 11: 269–338.

——(1921) 'Group Psychology and the Analysis of the Ego', SE 18: 65–143; PFL 12: 91–178.

——(1923) 'The Ego and the Id', SE 19: 1–66: PFL 11: 339–406.

——(1925a) 'An Autobiographical Study', SE 20: 3–74; PFL 15: 185–260.

——(1925b) 'Some Psychical Consequences of the Anatomical Distinction between the Sexes', SE 19: 241–58; PFL 7: 323–43.

——(1927a) 'The Future of an Illusion', SE 21: 1–56; PFL 12: 181–241.

——(1927b) 'Fetishism', SE 21: 147–57; PFL 12: 181–241.

——(1928) 'Dostoevsky and Parricide', SE 21: 173–94; PFL 14: 435–60.

——(1930) *Civilization and its Discontents*, SE 21: 57–145; PFL 12: 243–340.

——(1938) *An Outline of Psychoanalysis*, SE 23: 139–207; PFL 15: 371–444.

——(1939) 'Moses and Monotheism', SE 23: 1–137; PFL 13: 237–386.

SECONDARY TEXTS

Appignanesi, L. and Forrester, J. (1992) *Freud's Women*, London: Virago.

Appignanesi, R. and Zarate, O. (1999) *Introducing Freud*, Cambridge: Icon Books.

Auden, W.H. (1976) 'In Memory of Sigmund Freud', in E. Mendelson (ed.) *Collected Poems*, London: Faber.

Barthes, R. (1995) 'The Death of the Author', in S. Burke (ed.) *Authorship: From Plato to the Postmodern: A Reader*, Edinburgh: Edinburgh University Press, 125–30.

de Beauvoir, S. ([1949] 1972) *The Second Sex*, trans. H.M. Parshley, Harmondsworth: Penguin.

Bergner, G. (2005) *Taboo Subjects: Race, Sex and Psychoanalysis*, Minneapolis MN: University of Minnesota Press.

Berman, J. (1985) *The Talking Cure: Literary Representations of Psychoanalysis*, New York: New York University Press.

Bernheimer, C. and Kahane, C. (eds) (1985) *In Dora's Case: Freud–Hysteria–Feminism*, London: Virago.

Bland, L. and Doan L. (eds) (1998) *Sexology Uncensored: The Documents of Social Science*, Cambridge: Polity Press.

Bloom, H. (1973) *The Anxiety of Influence: A Theory of Poetry*, New York: Oxford University Press.

Bonaparte, M. (1949) *The Life and Works of Edgar Allan Poe*, London: Imago.

Bowie, M. (1991) *Lacan*, London: Harvard University Press.

Bowlby, R. (2007) *Freudian Mythologies: Greek Tragedy and Modern Identities*, Oxford: Oxford University Press.

Brennan, T. (ed.) (1989) *Between Feminism and Psychoanalysis*, London and New York: Routledge.

Brooks, P. (1985) *Reading for the Plot: Design and Intention in Narrative*, New York: Vintage.

——(1988) 'The Idea of a Psychoanalytic Literary Criticism', in F. Meltzer (ed.) *The Trial(s) of Psychoanalysis*, Chicago: University of Chicago Press, 39–64.

Burgin, V., Donald, J., and Kaplan C. (eds) (1986) *Formations of Fantasy*, London: Routledge.

Butler, J. (1990) *Gender Trouble: Feminism and the Subversion of Identity*, New York: Routledge.

——(1993) *Bodies that Matter: On the Discursive Limits of 'Sex'*, New York: Routledge.

——(1997) *The Psychic Life of Power: Theories in Subjection*, Stanford CA: Stanford University Press.

Crews, F. *et al.* (1995) *The Memory Wars: Freud's Legacy in Dispute*, New York: New York Review of Books.

Davidson, A.I. (1988) 'How to Do the History of Psychoanalysis: a Reading of Freud's *Three Essays on the Theory of Sexuality*', in F. Meltzer (ed.) *The Trial(s) of Psychoanalysis*, Chicago: University of Chicago Press, 39–64.

Derrida, J. (1978) 'Freud and the Scene of Writing', in *Writing and Difference*, trans. A. Bass, London: Routledge, 196–230.

——(1987) *The Postcard: From Socrates to Freud and Beyond*, trans. A. Bass, Chicago: University of Chicago Press.

Doane, M. (1991) *Femmes fatales: Feminism, Film Theory, Psychoanalysis*, London: Routledge.

Dufresne, T. (ed.) (2004) *Killing Freud: Twentieth Century Culture and the Death of Psychoanalysis*, London: Continuum.

Edwards, J. (2008) *Eve Kosofsky Sedgwick*, London: Routledge.

Ellmann, M. (ed.) (1994) *Psychoanalytic Literary Criticism*, London: Longman.

Falkland, G. (2000) *Freud's Literary Culture*, Cambridge: Cambridge University Press.

Fanon, F. (1986) *Black Skin, White Masks*, London: Pluto.

Feldstein, R. and Sussman, H. (eds) (1990) *Psychoanalysis and ...* , London: Routledge.

Felman, S. (1977a) 'To Open the Question', *Yale French Studies*, 55/56: 5–10.

——(1977b) 'Turning the Screw of Interpretation', *Yale French Studies*, 55/56: 94–207.

Fish, S. (1988) 'Withholding the Missing Portion: Psychoanalysis and Rhetoric', in F. Meltzer (ed.) *The Trial(s) of Psychoanalysis*, Chicago: University of Chicago Press, 183–210.

Forrester, J. (1990) *The Seductions of Psychoanalysis: Freud, Lacan, and Derrida*, Cambridge: Cambridge University Press.

——(1997) *Dispatches from the Freud War: Psychoanalysis and its Passions*, Cambridge MA: Harvard University Press.

Foucault, M. (1990) *The History of Sexuality*, Vol. I, trans. R. Hurley, London: Penguin.

Frazer, J. (1993) *The Golden Bough*, Ware: Wordsworth Editions.

Gallop, J. (1982) *The Daughter's Seduction: Feminism and Psychoanalysis*, Ithaca NY: Cornell University Press.

Gay, P. (1989) *Freud: A Life for our Time*, London: Macmillan.

Greedharry, M. (2008) *Postcolonial Theory and Psychoanalysis: From Uneasy Engagements to Effective Critique*, London: Palgrave.

Grosz, E. (1990) *Jacques Lacan: A Feminist Introduction*, London: Routledge.

Gunn, D. (1988) *Psychoanalysis and Fiction*, Cambridge: Cambridge University Press.

Hall, S. (1996) 'The After-life of Frantz Fanon: Why Fanon? Why Now? Why *Black Skin, White Masks*?', in A. Read (ed.) *The Fact of Blackness: Frantz Fanon and Visual Representation*, Seattle WA: Bay Press.

Heath, S. (1986) 'Joan Riviere and the Masquerade', in V. Burgin, J. Donald and C. Kaplan (eds) *Formations of Fantasy*, London: Routledge, 45–61.

Hoffmann, E.T.A. (1982) *Tales of Hoffmann*, trans. R.J. Hollingdale, London: Penguin.

Jacobus, M. (1996) *First Things: The Maternal Imaginary in Literature, Art and Psychoanalysis*, London and New York: Routledge.

——(2005) *The Poetics of Psychoanalysis: In the Wake of Klein*, Oxford: Oxford University Press.

Jones, E. (1953–57) *Sigmund Freud: Life and Works*, Vols I–III, London: Hogarth Press.

Katz, J.N. (1997) '"Homosexual" and "Heterosexual": Questioning the Terms', in M. Duberman (ed.) *A Queer World: The Center for Lesbian and Gay Studies Reader*, New York: New York University Press.

Klein, M. (1985) *The Selected Melanie Klein*, ed. Juliet Mitchell, London: Penguin Books.

Kristeva, J. (1980) *Desire in Language: A Semiotic Approach to Literature and Art*, trans T. Gorz, A. Jardine and L. Roudiez, Oxford: Blackwell.

——(1982) *Powers of Horror: An Essay on Abjection*, trans. L. Roudiez, New York: Columbia University Press.

——(1989) *Black Sun: Depression and Melancholia*, trans. L. Roudiez, New York: Columbia University Press.

Lacan, J. (1977) *Ecrits: A Selection*, trans. A. Sheridan, New York: Norton.

——(1988) *The Seminar of Jacques Lacan*, Book II, *The Ego in Freud's Theory and in the Technique of Psychoanalysis, 1954–1955*, trans. S. Tomaselli, ed. J.-A. Miller, Cambridge: Cambridge University Press.

Lane, C. (ed.) (1998) *The Psychoanalysis of Race*, New York: Columbia University Press.

Laplanche, J. and Pontalis, J.-B. (1973) *The Language of Psychoanalysis*, trans. D. Nicholson-Smith, New York: Norton.

——(1986) 'Fantasy and the Origins of Sexuality', in V. Burgin, J. Donald and C. Kaplan (eds) *Formations of Fantasy*, London: Routledge.

Lebeau, V. (2001) *Psychoanalysis and Cinema: The Play of Shadows*, London: Wallflower Press.

Lesser, R.C. and Schoenberg, E. (eds) (1999) *That Obscure Object of Desire: Freud's Female Homosexual Revisited*, New York: Routledge.

Mahony, P.J. (1987) *Freud as a Writer*, New Haven CT: Yale University Press.

Marcus, Laura (ed.) (1999) *Sigmund Freud's* The Interpretation of Dreams: *New Interdisciplinary Essays*, Manchester: Manchester University Press.

Masson, J. (1984) *The Assault on Truth: Freud's Suppression of the Seduction Theory*, New York: Farrar Straus & Giroux.

——(ed.) (1985) *The Complete Letters of Sigmund Freud to Wilhelm Fliess, 1887–1904*, Cambridge MA: Harvard University Press.

Meisel, P. (2002) *The Literary Freud*, London: Routledge.

Meltzer, F. (ed.) (1988) *The Trial(s) of Psychoanalysis*, Chicago: University of Chicago Press.

Mitchell, J. (1974) *Psychoanalysis and Feminism: Freud, Reich, Lang and Women*, New York: Pantheon.

Mitchell, J. and Rose, J. (eds) (1985) *Feminine Sexuality: Jacques Lacan and the École freudienne*, New York: Norton.

Moi, T. (1985) *Sexual/Textual Politics: Feminist Literary Theory*, London: Methuen.

Mulvey, L. (1989) *Visual and other Pleasures*, Basingstoke: Macmillan.

Neu, J. (ed.) (1991) *The Cambridge Companion to Freud*, Cambridge: Cambridge University Press.

Penley, C. (ed.) (1988) *Feminism and Film Theory*, London: Routledge.

Phillips, A. (1993) *On Kissing, Tickling and Being Bored*, Cambridge MA: Harvard University Press.

——(1994) *On Flirtation*, London: Faber.

——(2000) *Promises, Promises*, London: Faber.

Phillips, J. and Stonebridge, L. (eds) (1998) *Reading Melanie Klein*, London and New York: Routledge.

Rank, O. (1971) *The Double: A Psychoanalytic Study*, Chapel Hill NC: University of North Carolina Press.

Rieff, P. (1959) *Freud: The Mind of the Moralist*, Chicago: University of Chicago Press.

Riviere, J. (1986) 'Womanliness as Masquerade', in V. Burgin, J. Donald and C. Kaplan (eds) *Formations of Fantasy*, London: Routledge.

Rose, J. (1986) *Sexuality in the Field of Vision*, London: Verso.

——(1991) *The Haunting of Sylvia Plath*, London: Virago.

——(1993) *Why War? Psychoanalysis, Politics and the Return to Melanie Klein*, Oxford: Blackwell.

——(2003) *On Not Being Able to Sleep: Psychoanalysis and the Modern World*, London: Chatto & Windus.

——(2007) *The Last Resistance*, London: Verso.

Royle, N. (2003) *The Uncanny*, Manchester: Manchester University Press.

Salih, S. (2002) *Judith Butler*, London: Routledge.

Sedgwick, E.K. (1985) *Between Men: English Literature and Male Homosocial Desire*, New York: Columbia University Press.

——(1990) *The Epistemology of the Closet*, London: Penguin.

Showalter, E. (1985) *The Female Malady: Women, Madness, and English Culture, 1830–1980*, New York: Penguin.

Smith-Rosenberg, C. (1985) 'The Hysterical Woman', in *Disorderly Conduct: Visions of Gender in Victorian America*, New York: Knopf.

Storr, A. (1989) *Freud*, Oxford: Oxford University Press.

Surprenant, C. (2008) *Freud: A Guide for the Perplexed*, London: Continuum.

Vice, S. (ed.) (1996) *Psychoanalytic Criticism: A Reader*, Cambridge: Polity Press.

Walton, J. (2001) *Fair Sex, Savage Dreams: Race, Psychoanalysis, Sexual Difference*, Durham NC: Duke University Press.

Warner, M. (1990) 'Homo-narcissism: or, Heterosexuality', in J. Boone and M. Cadden (eds) *Engendering Men: The Question of Male Feminist Criticism*, London: Routledge.

Weeks, J. (1980) *Sexuality and its Discontents: Meanings, Myths and Modern Sexualities*, London: Longman.

Wollheim, R. (1971) *Freud*, Glasgow: Fontana.

——(1991) 'Freud and the Understanding of Art', in Jerome Neu (ed.) *The Cambridge Companion to Freud*, Cambridge: Cambridge University Press.

Wordsworth, W. (1970) *The Prelude*, ed. E. de Selincourt, Oxford: Oxford University Press.

Wright, E. (1984) *Psychoanalytic Criticism: Theory in Practice*, London: Methuen.

Žižek, S. (1989) *The Sublime Object of Ideology*, London: Verso.

INDEX

Page numbers in **bold** denote highlighted boxed section on subject.

eBooks – at www.eBookstore.tandf.co.uk

A library at your fingertips!

eBooks are electronic versions of printed books. You can store them on your PC/laptop or browse them online.

They have advantages for anyone needing rapid access to a wide variety of published, copyright information.

eBooks can help your research by enabling you to bookmark chapters, annotate text and use instant searches to find specific words or phrases. Several eBook files would fit on even a small laptop or PDA.

NEW: Save money by eSubscribing: cheap, online access to any eBook for as long as you need it.
Annual subscription packages

We now offer special low-cost bulk subscriptions to packages of eBooks in certain subject areas. These are available to libraries or to individuals.

For more information please contact
webmaster.ebooks@tandf.co.uk

We're continually developing the eBook concept, so keep up to date by visiting the website.

www.eBookstore.tandf.co.uk

THE NEW CRITICAL IDIOM

Series Editor: John Drakakis, University of Stirling

The New Critical Idiom is an invaluable series of introductory guides to today's critical terminology. Each book:

- provides a handy, explanatory guide to the use (and abuse) of the term
- offers an original and distinctive overview by a leading literary and cultural critic
- relates the term to the larger field of cultural representation.

With a strong emphasis on clarity, lively debate and the widest possible breadth of examples, *The New Critical Idiom* is an indispensable approach to key topics in literary studies.

'*The New Critical Idiom* is a constant resource – essential reading for all students.'

Tom Paulin, University of Oxford

'Easily the most informative and wide-ranging series of its kind, so packed with bright ideas that it has become an indispensable resource for students of literature.'

Terry Eagleton, University of Manchester

Related titles available in this series:

Sexuality by Joseph Bristow

Joseph Bristow introduces readers to the most influential contemporary theories of sexual desire and reveals how nineteenth century scientists invented 'sexuality'. This clear and fascinating introductory guide makes complex theoretical ideas accessible to readers of all levels.

ISBN 13: 978-0-415-12268-9 (HBK)
ISBN 13: 978-0-415-08494-9 (PBK)
ISBN 13: 978-0-203-12976-0 (EBK)

The Unconscious by Antony Easthope

The unconscious is a term which is central to the understanding of psychoanalysis, and, indeed everyday life. In this introductory guide, Antony Easthope provides a witty and accessible overview of the subject showing the reality of the unconscious with a startling variety of examples.

ISBN 13: 978-0-415-19208-8 (HBK)
ISBN 13: 978-0-415-19209-5 (PBK)
ISBN 13: 978-0-203-19765-3 (EBK)

For further information on individual books in the series, visit: www.routledgeliterature.com